Junior Great Books

SERIES 7

The Reader Writes

The Great Books Foundation
A nonprofit educational organization

DEVELOPMENT TEAM

Margo M. Criscuola
Nora Palmieri
Mike Wolfkiel

ADVISORY TEAM

Michael Cannon, El Paso Independent School District, El Paso, Texas
Kimberly Fowler, Traner Middle School, Reno, Nevada
Judy Gasser, Grand Prairie Independent School District, Grand Prairie, Texas
Judith Kelly, Educational Service Center, Fort Worth, Texas
Adrienne Robb-Fund, Wantagh Elementary School, Wantagh, New York

9 8 7 6 5 4 3 2 1

Printed in the United States of America

Published and distributed by

The Great Books Foundation
A nonprofit educational organization

35 East Wacker Drive, Suite 2300
Chicago, IL 60601-2298

www.greatbooks.org

DESIGN William Seabright & Associates
COVER ART Ed Young
INTERIOR ART William Seabright
CALLIGRAPHY Linda Helton

Introduction

The Junior Great Books approach to writing about literature starts with curiosity and insightful questions about something you have read. For example, consider this short poem by Edna St. Vincent Millay:

> *Safe upon the solid rock the ugly houses stand:*
> *Come and see my shining palace built upon the sand!*

If you had to say what this poem means, you could probably come up with a sentence or two right away. The poet is making a contrast between ugly houses built on solid rock and her own "shining palace" built on sand; she may really be talking about two different ways to live.

Now try asking questions about some aspect of the poem, such as *Why does the poet call the houses ugly? What's wrong with being safe? Is there any way the "shining palace" the poet describes can be made to last, or does it shine precisely because it is a temporary thing? Why does the poet want someone to come and see her palace? Whom is she trying to convince?* There's no one right answer to any of these questions, but certain answers will make more sense to you than others. Thinking about these questions, and those of your classmates, can help you see more in the poem than you did before.

This is the part of the writing process laid out in the QUESTIONS stage of *The Reader Writes*. In this first stage, you will be asking questions, sharing questions with others, comparing possible answers, and writing about them. You'll learn specific strategies for doing these things well, demonstrated with examples based on the selections in Junior Great Books Series 7.

The Writer's Road Map illustrates the entire writing process in three stages: QUESTIONS, ISSUES, and POSITIONS. You start with your own questions about what you read, because a strong question forms the core of a worthwhile piece of writing. Then you develop issues—the divergent possible answers an interesting question might have and the reasons and evidence that make them convincing. Finally, you take a position—a full, well-supported idea that in your mind is the best solution to your chosen question.

At each stage you will write essays, and as you learn more of the strategies presented, your essays will become more focused, better developed, more convincing. At every stage you will build on your own curiosity by considering and responding to the ideas of your classmates in shared inquiry discussion.

Writing about literature is an important part of this development for two reasons. First, literature is a great source of insight into life. A good work of literature represents the problems all human beings face, without trying to solve them for us. In short, it offers a lot to write about. Second, literature gives us a shared experience. Sharing your questions and possible answers with classmates is a sure way to increase and strengthen them. But to discuss ideas in depth, you and your classmates must share experience in detail. Personal experiences are all different and often are not easy to explain to others, but literature provides an experience that everyone in the class can tap into directly.

The Reader Writes incorporates all of the traditionally recognized steps of the writing process—generating ideas, planning, drafting, revising, publishing—but with a difference. The Great Books approach places a strong emphasis on the first two steps, generating ideas and planning ways to support them. These are the steps in which you come up with something unique and substantial to say, something only you can write. *The Reader Writes* will help you do this deliberately and with confidence. The results will be lively essays that voice your convictions and illuminate for others the literature you write about.

The Reader Writes

The Writer's Road Map

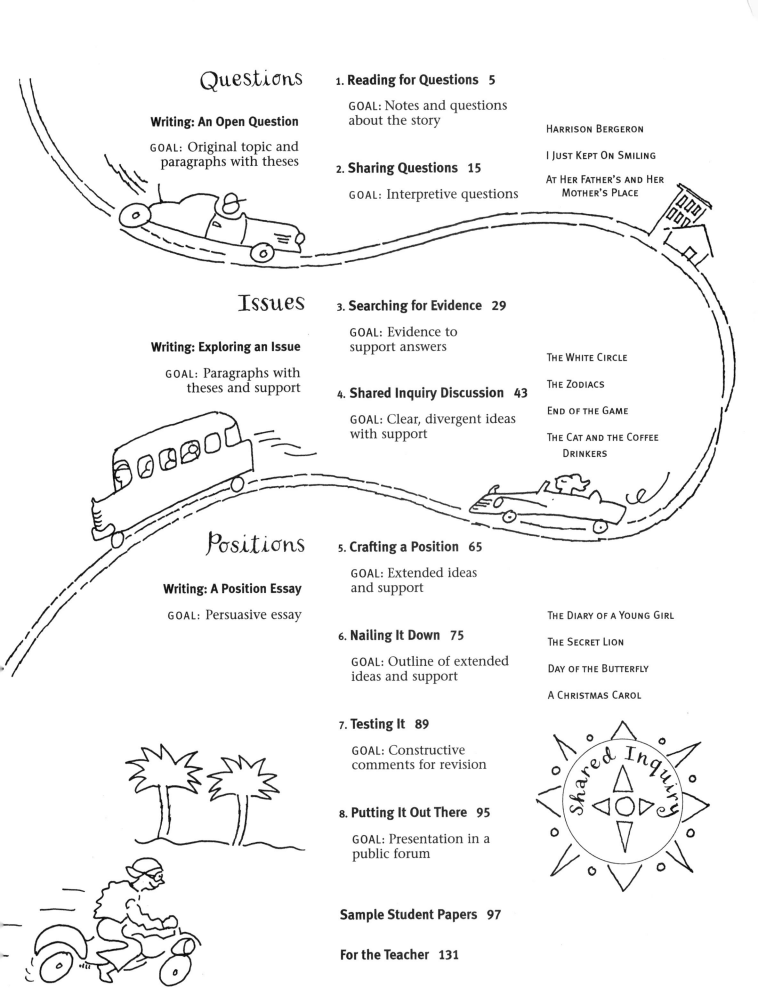

Questions

Writing: An Open Question

GOAL: Original topic and paragraphs with theses

HARRISON BERGERON

I JUST KEPT ON SMILING

AT HER FATHER'S AND HER
MOTHER'S PLACE

Issues

Writing: Exploring an Issue

GOAL: Paragraphs with theses and support

THE WHITE CIRCLE

THE ZODIACS

END OF THE GAME

THE CAT AND THE COFFEE
DRINKERS

Positions

Writing: A Position Essay

GOAL: Persuasive essay

THE DIARY OF A YOUNG GIRL

THE SECRET LION

DAY OF THE BUTTERFLY

A CHRISTMAS CAROL

Shared Inquiry

Questions

When invited to share your honest responses to a thought-provoking piece of literature, chances are you find yourself asking questions. As a reader, you can use these questions to build your own ideas about a story; as a writer, you can use them to present your unique point of view to others.

In QUESTIONS, you'll turn your puzzlement, frustration, or enjoyment of a story into fruitful questions. You'll then write a short essay about your favorite question, proposing and explaining several possible answers.

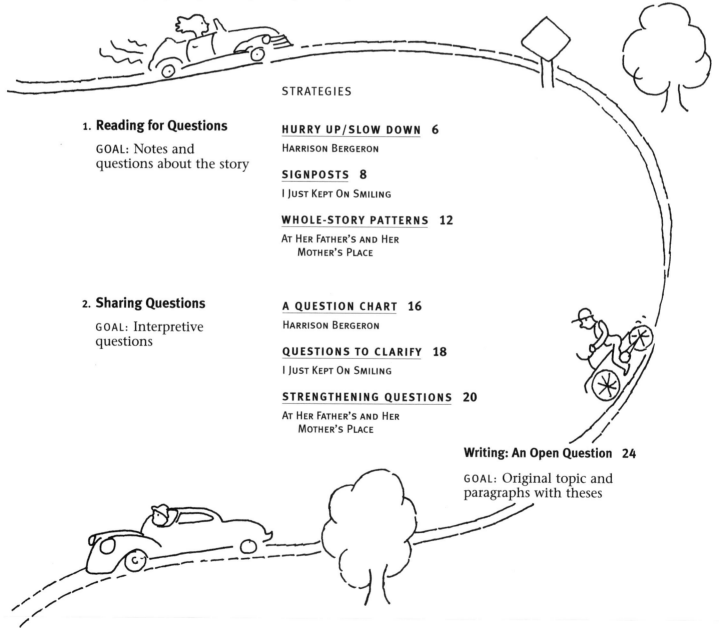

1 Reading for Questions

When you ask questions as you read, you are approaching a work of literature with curiosity and confidence. Often questions will come to you spontaneously, prompted by something in the story that you didn't expect or don't understand.

YOU MIGHT ASK

*   Why did things turn out this way?

*   Why did this character do or say that?

*   Why was the tone—the "sound" of the words on the page—the way it was?

*   Why was such a character or such an incident included? What did it contribute to the story?

You can also use strategies, like the ones on the next few pages, to identify questions in passages where there are shifts in meaning or where you and other readers interpret things differently.

THE QUESTION THAT YOU'LL EVENTUALLY WANT TO THINK, TALK, AND WRITE ABOUT WILL BE

*   Genuine—the question really puzzles you

*   Specific—the question could only be asked about this story

*   Clear—the question is unambiguous

*   Interesting—the question seems worth further thought

For now, though, just aim to take rough notes on the stories and write lots of questions. This is the time for exploring.

Reading for Questions

Have you ever carried something very heavy and found yourself walking much faster than usual? A similar thing can happen as you read something challenging. You may find yourself plunging ahead quickly when things don't make sense, hoping that when you see the whole you'll be able to pull it all together. This hurry-up approach works. So does slowing down over the parts that give you trouble, to look at them closely and mull them over.

Pay attention to how you feel as you read. Be ready to hurry up or slow down when you feel any of the following:

Uneasy or confused—something doesn't seem to follow or fit together

Annoyed or troubled—something seems wrong or ugly

Pleased or impressed—something seems beautiful, true, or distinctive

Surprised—something unexpected happens

Your goal is to write lots of questions about the text, so problems are good! For now, just identify the problems clearly enough to save them for future consideration.

WHEN YOU HURRY UP, TRY THIS METHOD:

* Mark the place in the text that triggered your feeling.

* Go back to the beginning of that passage and read through it quickly.

* Explain the passage to yourself to see if you've got it.

* If you still feel stumped, repeat steps 1–3.

* If the passage still seems strange, write a question about it in your journal.

WHEN YOU SLOW DOWN, TRY THIS:

* Mark the words and passages that triggered your feeling or note them (with the page numbers) in your journal.

* Think over each one.

* Jot down your ideas in a few words or as a question in your journal.

* Read on, looking for more pieces of the puzzle.

Reading for Questions

DEMO: THE SLOW-DOWN APPROACH

Here are one reader's notes and questions after using the slow-down approach for a passage from "Harrison Bergeron." Try adding your own.

> "You been so tired lately—kind of wore out," said Hazel. "If there was just some way we could make a little hole in the bottom of the bag, and just take out a few of them lead balls. Just a few."
>
> "Two years in prison and two thousand dollars fine for every ball I took out," said George. "I don't call that a bargain."
>
> "If you could just take a few out when you came home from work," said Hazel. "I mean—you don't compete with anybody around here. You just set around."
>
> "If I tried to get away with it," said George, "then other people'd get away with it— and pretty soon we'd be right back to the dark ages again, with everybody competing against everybody else. You wouldn't like that, would you?"
>
> "I'd hate it," said Hazel.
>
> "There you are," said George. "The minute people start cheating on laws, what do you think happens to society?"
>
> If Hazel hadn't been able to come up with an answer to this question, George couldn't have supplied one. A siren was going off in his head.

Tired lately—anything special happening to George recently?

George—the smart one—thinks it's right to wear the handicap bag!

Competition = dark ages? Is George supposed to be right about this?

Can't answer his question. Is all his thinking wrecked by his handicaps— or are we supposed to agree that it would be bad to go back to competition?

Reading for Questions

Signposts are details you notice at the beginning of a story that turn out to be important later. If you focus on them right away, you will better understand later developments. Signposts to look for include

* Characters' odd or special characteristics. How will they play out in later incidents?

* Actions that could have dramatic or serious consequences. What will happen as a result?

* A tone or mood that seems distinctive or strange. Will it deepen or change?

* Remarks by the author that sum things up or state an opinion. Should we agree with them or challenge them later in the story?

After reading the first two or three pages of a story, look back and choose the signposts that you want to track. Jot down each one and include why you noticed them, so you'll know just what you're looking for as you read on.

WHEN WORKING WITH SIGNPOSTS

* Work with several, since some will fizzle out.

* Take notes as you see things related to your signposts. If you use a code word or an icon for each signpost, your notes can be short.

* If some signposts don't seem to relate to later parts of the story, drop them and try new ones.

* When you finish reading, look back over your notes and write in your journal the questions they suggest to you.

Reading for Questions

DEMO: **SIGNPOSTS**

Here are four signposts one reader identified in the opening pages of "I Just Kept On Smiling." The first signpost related to later developments in the story. The second one fizzled out. Try filling in the missing elements of the last two signposts. Do they relate to later developments or fizzle out?

SIGNPOST:

Smiling—title and p. 10: "Dom Gilbert waited, so I smiled at him."

WHY IT'S A SIGNPOST:

Usually people smile because they want to, not because someone else waited. Why does he smile? Does he always smile deliberately?

LOOK FOR:

Other places in the story where he smiles

LATER NOTE:

p. 15: "I felt him looking at me about halfway through the lesson. I looked up and smiled, and he turned away"—again smiling as a way to make someone "go away."

SIGNPOST:

He doesn't tell anyone it's his birthday, and he throws away the birthday cards.

WHY IT'S A SIGNPOST:

Birthdays are days to celebrate yourself. Usually people want others to know about their birthdays. Why doesn't he feel like that?

LOOK FOR:

Are there "many happy returns" of his birthday? Does something special happen because it's his birthday?

LATER NOTE:

No more mention of his birthday! No one besides his family and his teacher brings it up.

SIGNPOST:

Takes exercise books from the teacher's desk.

WHY IT'S A SIGNPOST:

LOOK FOR:

What does he want the exercise books for? Why does he take them? Are there consequences?

LATER NOTE:

SIGNPOST:

Has the same blah tone when talking about his birthday, about taking the exercise books, and about schoolwork.

WHY IT'S A SIGNPOST:

LOOK FOR:

Will anything happen to make him feel something?

LATER NOTE:

Reading for Questions

Use this organizer in your journal to note and track your own signposts.

SIGNPOST: _____

_____

_____

WHY IT'S A SIGNPOST: _____

_____

_____

_____

_____

LOOK FOR: _____

_____

LATER NOTE: _____

_____

_____

_____

_____

_____

Reading for Questions

STRATEGY: **WHOLE-STORY PATTERNS**

Patterns encourage you to compare things. When you compare elements that create a pattern in a story, you may uncover questions—either because you find things that are unexpectedly the same or because you find them unexpectedly different.

COMMON PATTERNS TO LOOK FOR ARE

* A repeated word or phrase

* A repeated action, by the same character in a different way, or by a different character

* A resemblance between one character, place, or action and another

After you've read a story, think of a large pattern it presents. Set up a comparison chart to sort it out. Go back and look at the pattern in greater detail and list its elements in your chart. Is the pattern consistent? Are there breaks in it? Ask questions based on consistencies or surprising breaks.

Reading for Questions

DEMO: **WHOLE-STORY PATTERNS**

In "At Her Father's and Her Mother's Place," one clear pattern is that there are two parents and two households. It seems natural to compare them. This reader used a comparison chart with two columns. Add your own comparisons, then use them to help you think of additional questions about the story.

	AT HER FATHER'S PLACE	AT HER MOTHER'S PLACE
What Talya does	Reads, looks at magazines, homework / Wants to ask why he left, but can't	Cleans up, cooks / Asks why father left (mother won't tell)
What the place is like	"windows looked out on to three corners of the world"	"windows looked out on to blind, brick walls" "everything so horrible"
What her parent does	Draws, writes	Helps people
Why Talya likes it	"Like vacation"	?

1. Why does it say "three corners of the world"? Does Talya's father show her more of the world than her mother does?

2. Why does Talya clean up her mother's place and put a tablecloth on the table?

3. Is the story saying that Talya's mother is better than her father? Does Talya think that?

4. _____

5. _____

6. _____

2 Sharing Questions

When you share your questions about a story with other
readers, some new questions will occur to you and
some of your initial questions will be answered. In the
process, you will see three different kinds of questions.

Factual questions are used up quickly. A single answer,
based on information in the story, will satisfy you
and resolve the problem. You will no longer feel any
curiosity about it.

STARTING POINT

Notes and questions
about the story

GOAL

Interpretive
questions

Evaluative questions can only be answered if you look to your own
experiences or if you speculate, adding things the story does not tell you.
These questions take you beyond the story.

Interpretive questions demand more thought. You and other readers will see
several possible answers that will then lead you to new ideas about the story.
They are difficult, but rewarding. Interpretive questions are your goal in
Sharing Questions.

In Sharing Questions, brainstorm questions with your group and write them
down, preferably on the board so the whole group can see them.

TRY

* Using questions you wrote in Reading for Questions

* Sharing the notes you took in Reading for Questions—others might
  see questions in them

* Looking back on the story as a whole and offering second thoughts

Next, suggest several possible answers to these questions. Where do these
questions lead you? Do your answers suggest additional, interpretive questions?
If so, write the interpretive questions that most interest you in your journal.

As you work through Sharing Questions with your group, try the strategies
on the following pages to organize your group's responses and generate
interpretive questions.

Sharing Questions

A question chart can help your class keep track of those questions that interest you. On the board, write your initial questions in the first column. In the next column, write your first take—the first possible answers you and your group suggest. You might remember a place in the story that helps you answer a question, or you might bring up an answer that just came to you. Try to do both.

For the third column, your second take, look over your group's first-take answers and reconsider the question. Is it still a question for you? If it's been answered or it seems to be going nowhere, drop it and mark an *X* in the third column. If it's still a question, try to state why it still interests you.

Finally, compare your questions with your second-take answers. Can you rewrite any of the questions or add to them so that they include your thinking so far? If so, make one of these your interpretive question, the one you'll write about in your essay.

Sharing Questions

DEMO: **A QUESTION CHART**

Here is one class's question chart from "Harrison Bergeron." Try completing the chart for the questions given.

QUESTION	FIRST TAKE (possible answers)	SECOND TAKE (reconsider the question)	INTERPRETIVE QUESTION
IS DIANA MOON GLAMPERS SUPPOSED TO BE A FUNNY NAME?	Yes, "Glampers" is kind of dumb. So is "Hazel."	Dumb people rule in this society; it's not really equal.	Is this equality or a chance for the dumb to rule the smart?
	Beautiful names are unequal.	X	
	Yes, and Hazel says and does funny things—"doozy." (pp. 3, 9)	Hazel is funny, but her own son is getting killed.	Why are parts of the story funny when it ends so sadly?
WHAT DOES "H-G MEN" MEAN?	They work for the Handicapper General (p.1); put on handicaps (p.5).	X	
HOW CAN A FOURTEEN-YEAR-OLD BE SEVEN FEET TALL AND CARRY 300 POUNDS?	It's supposed to be exaggerated, kind of funny.		
	Maybe in 2081 everyone is bigger and stronger.	X	
	He's a "genius and athlete" (p. 5).		
	If you carry weights, and then get rid of them, you might be stronger.	But the weights are to keep you from being superior—not to make you stronger.	Are we supposed to think that Harrison's handicaps made him stronger?
WHY DOES HARRISON DANCE WITH THE BALLERINA ON TV?	TV is the way to reach people. "Watch me" (p. 6)	He's sure to get caught. It seems foolish.	
	He wants to enjoy being "what he can become." (p. 6)	The dance is beautiful, though it can't last long.	
	He wants to show people the beauty of inequality.	Parents don't get the message.	
WHAT ARE ALL THOSE OTHER AMENDMENTS TO THE CONSTITUTION?	Maybe the government got taken over by a weird political party that. . . . Don't know. Doesn't say in the story.	X	

Sharing Questions

STRATEGY: <u>**QUESTIONS TO CLARIFY**</u>

When you and your classmates share questions and suggest answers in your group, you are thinking on your feet. You can't always be sure where your ideas are going. So, if you don't understand something, try following up with a question or two.

Reporters, scientists, lawyers, psychologists, business people, and teachers all use questioning as a direct route to learning more. You can, too. Your questions can also help the other person get a firmer grip on a slippery new idea. Asking what someone means shows that you value his or her ideas.

WHEN ASKING QUESTIONS TO CLARIFY AND EXPLAIN SOMEONE'S THINKING

* Listen to the other person carefully, with an open mind.

* Check your understanding of what he or she said. Are there gaps? Places where you got lost?

* Ask about something specific, to give the other person a clear starting point.

* If you can't be specific, ask the person to repeat his or her answer but in a different way.

* Question respectfully. Show that you will consider the response seriously.

* Don't help out or put words in other people's mouths. Let them think for themselves.

* Let others try answering your question too, to get their take on the idea.

Sharing Questions

DEMO: **QUESTIONS TO CLARIFY**

These statements from a group discussion of "I Just Kept On Smiling" sounded different at first, but in fact they are similar.

ANSWER 1: NICKY CARVER AND THE NARRATOR REALLY HAVE A LOT IN COMMON.

What do they have in common?

THEY'RE BOTH OUTSIDERS. THE NARRATOR IS AN OUTSIDER BECAUSE HE DOESN'T LIKE ANYONE, AND NICKY IS AN OUTSIDER BECAUSE HE'S REALLY MUCH NICER THAN ANYONE.

ANSWER 2: NICKY CARVER IS THE COMPLETE OPPOSITE OF THE NARRATOR.

Opposite—how?

NICKY REALLY WANTS TO BE GOOD AND HONEST. THE NARRATOR LOOKS DOWN ON EVERYONE, EVEN NICKY.

These statements from the same discussion sounded similar, but they are different. Following up with clarifying questions helped to distinguish them.

ANSWER 1: NICKY CONFESSES SO HE CAN BE BETTER THAN THE NARRATOR.

How does confessing make him better?

NICKY IS MAKING THE THIEF NOT ENJOY STEALING ANYMORE. HE'S SHAMING HIM INTO CHANGING HIS WAYS. BUT HE'S NOT BEING A BULLY LIKE PIGGOTT AND THOSE BOYS, OR A TATTLETALE.

ANSWER 2: NICKY WANTS TO SHOW THE NARRATOR HE'S BETTER, TO PUT HIM DOWN.

Put him down?

SHOW HIM HOW A REALLY BRAVE PERSON WOULD BEHAVE. HE WOULD TAKE CREDIT FOR BEING A THIEF. HE WOULD FLAUNT BEING BAD.

Try this strategy in your own Sharing Questions discussion. Follow up others' comments with your own clarifying questions or try out some of these:

What did you mean by "_____"?

Is that sort of like "_____"?

Can you tell me more about what you said, "_____"?

I'm not sure I got that. Could you repeat your answer?

Sharing Questions

Sharing Questions can lead you to deeper, more challenging questions than those you asked at first. Look over your initial questions and ask

* What did we mean by this question?

* Do these two questions point to a third, larger question?

* Do these interesting answers point to a more interesting question?

* Do these dull answers suggest that our original question didn't get to what interested us in the first place?

As you develop these new questions, be sure they are interpretive questions with the following qualities:

* Genuine—the question really puzzles you.

* Specific—the question could only be asked about this story. Avoid general, all-purpose "literature" questions.

* Clear—the question is unambiguous. Avoid inside jokes, vague formulations, or loose metaphors.

* Interesting—the question seems worth further thought. It leads to several possible answers that affect how you see the plot and the main characters. Avoid private musings or wild conjectures.

Sharing Questions

DEMO: STRENGTHENING QUESTIONS

Here are three questions that didn't make it on to the Interpretive Question column of the chart below. Can you tell why they didn't make it? Can you turn one of them into a workable interpretive question to add to the chart?

IS TALYA'S MOTHER A SAINT?

WHAT IS THE MAIN CONFLICT IN THIS STORY?

WHY DID TALYA'S DAD STOP LOVING HER MOTHER?

QUESTION	FIRST TAKE (possible answers)	SECOND TAKE (reconsider the question)	INTERPRETIVE QUESTION
WHY DOES TALYA DECIDE TO LEAVE HER FATHER'S PLACE?	The love letter is "shameful" (p. 24). She feels her father has done wrong.	She loves "her father as well." (p. 32).	Why doesn't Talya tell her father about the letter?
	The letter says "our window."	Talya felt this window was her special link with her father (p. 20).	Why doesn't Talya tell her father why she wants to go back to her mother's place?
	Talya feels that if she stays she is keeping her father from being happy.	Wants to ask her father why he left (p. 23).	_____ _____ _____
WHY DID HER FATHER GET TALYA THE WATCH?	He loves Talya, and enjoys making her happy.	Any father would do this. But Talya wants to leave the watch at his place.	_____ _____ _____
	He likes nice things and he's used to them.	Mother won't give Talya skates; says she doesn't need them.	Are we supposed to think that Talya's mother is good, or that she's really too hard on herself and Talya?

Shared Inquiry Discussion

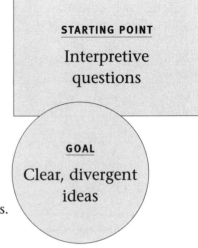

STARTING POINT

Interpretive questions

GOAL

Clear, divergent ideas

An interpretive question can be answered in more than one way—that's what makes it interesting. In QUESTIONS, shared inquiry discussion is a chance to loosen up your imagination and practice creating answers to questions and explaining them to others. You'll find that it makes you more quick to see questions as you read, too.

Remember to ask questions to clarify and distinguish answers. Your goal is a full and clear range of perspectives on the question being discussed.

HOW TO DO SHARED INQUIRY DISCUSSION

* The leader starts discussion with an interpretive question that stirs his or her genuine curiosity. A "further" question from Sharing Questions that has caught both the leader's and the participants' interest might be especially good.

* The leader and participants focus discussion on the story they have all read, rather than other books or personal experiences, so everyone is on equal footing.

* The leader only asks questions, so the participants can take the discussion where they want. Participants can ask questions when they wish.

* The goal of the discussion is for each participant to develop his or her own ideas about the question—not to reach a group consensus or conclusion.

Take a full class period for discussion—40 minutes at least—so everyone has an opportunity to speak several times. A small group—12 to 18—is most effective.

Building Your Answer

Before you begin discussion, write your answer to the leader's question—your own take on the question before being influenced by others' answers. Expect to clarify it in response to others' questions and to add to it or change it in response to others' opinions.

After discussion, write down other answers that interested you and that showed you why the discussion question was an open question. It's good practice for writing about your own question.

DISCUSSION QUESTION:

_____

_____

MY ANSWER BEFORE DISCUSSION:

_____

_____

_____

_____

_____

ADDITIONAL ANSWERS I HEARD IN DISCUSSION:

_____

_____

_____

_____

_____

Writing: An Open Question

STARTING POINT

Interpretive questions; clear, divergent ideas

GOAL

Original topic question and paragraphs with theses

ASSIGNMENT

In a short essay, propose several distinct possible answers to your favorite interpretive question from your journal.

AUDIENCE

Students who have not read the story or have read it only superficially.

PURPOSE

To get your readers interested in thinking further about the story.

FORMAT

In one to two typed, double-spaced pages

* State and clarify your interpretive question (one paragraph)

* Propose and explain your possible answers (one paragraph for each answer)

SHOW YOUR WORK

Along with your essay, turn in

* Your list of possible questions from Reading for Questions

* Your Question Chart from Sharing Questions

This is the first step toward a persuasive essay because you will

* Find a topic that can be looked at in more than one way

* See the strengths of alternative ideas

CONVENTIONS TO MASTER

* **Summarizing or paraphrasing passages from a story**

* **Maintaining a consistent verb tense throughout an essay**

For more guidance see the grading rubric on the facing page (p. 25) and the sample student papers for An Open Question (pp. 99–104).

Writing: An Open Question

CONTENT

EXPERT (5) The essay gives the reader an inviting, intriguing way to start thinking about the story.

* The topic question is clear, interesting, and seems important to understanding the story.

* Answers are distinct, and each opens up a new possible meaning of the story.

PRACTITIONER (3) The essay presents a question about the story and some possible answers.

* The topic question is related to the story, but it is rather simple or general, or not very clear.

* Answers are different from each other, but are rather simple or general and focus on the superficial meaning of the story.

BEGINNER (1) The essay lacks a clear question to explore; answers are weak.

* The topic question is vague, confusing, or could be asked about any story.

* Answers are unclear, far-fetched, or obvious, or repeat each other or are not directly related to the story.

ORGANIZATION

EXPERT (5) The topic question is explored in an orderly way, with each part of the essay making its own contribution to the exploration.

* The introduction opens the topic up and presents the question in a way that interests the reader.

* Each paragraph presents a different possible answer as its thesis and explains it.

PRACTITIONER (3) The topic question remains the focus throughout, but there are some gaps and repetition in the exploration of it.

* The introduction states the topic, but it is unclear or does not seem very interesting.

* Each paragraph presents a possible answer as its thesis and explains it. Some theses repeat earlier ideas, or some paragraphs restate theses instead of explaining them.

BEGINNER (1) The essay wanders or seems to lose track of the topic question; paragraphs leave ideas incomplete or repeat ideas.

* The introduction states the topic but may repeat it without explaining it.

* Paragraph theses are lacking or overly simple, they repeat the same idea, or several ideas are presented in a single sentence.

VOICE

EXPERT (5) The essay suggests an author who is genuinely curious about and engaged with the question.

PRACTITIONER (3) The essay suggests a sincere author who sometimes hesitates or falls back on conventional thinking.

BEGINNER (1) The essay suggests an author who is confused or just going through the motions.

WORD CHOICE

Apply your usual standards for word choice.

SENTENCE FLUENCY

Apply your usual standards for sentence fluency.

CONVENTIONS

Apply your usual standards for conventions.

PROCESS FOR THINKING AND WRITING

EXPERT (1) Full notes show the generation and development of the topic question and possible answers.

PRACTITIONER (3) Partial notes show some development of the topic question.

BEGINNER (1) Very few or no notes; a process cannot be traced.

Writing: An Open Question

STRATEGY: **THE FIVE-PARAGRAPH ESSAY**

You've probably learned about the five-paragraph essay. It's a good, simple model of how to organize a persuasive or informative essay:

> Paragraph 1—introduce the topic or thesis
>
> Paragraphs 2, 3, and 4—develop three specific aspects of the topic
>
> Paragraph 5—conclude

Why *three* paragraphs for development? Aiming for at least three helps you make sure you have a topic worth writing and reading about.

In your Open Question essay, your answers to your question will become the paragraphs of development. Test your favorite questions using the five-paragraph model below. Do you have at least two answers, each with several different key words and phrases?

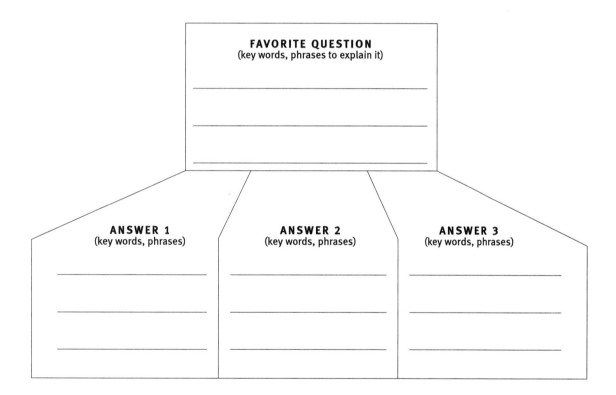

Now plan your essay, based on how many different answers you have. Experienced writers, of course, take as many paragraphs as they need to develop a topic.

Issues

You know how to ask interesting questions about a story. What's more, your questions have led you to some interesting answers. Now take it a step further—from a question with interesting possibilities to a question with convincing answers.

What kind of answer is convincing? Instead of "maybe's" and vague examples, evidence from the story—specific incidents or descriptions—backs up the idea. A question with one such answer, even if you disagree with it, sets you thinking. A question with several such answers, even (or especially!) if the answers differ, gives you a whole new way of making sense of the story. This kind of question is more than a simple query; it's an issue.

ISSUES takes up where QUESTIONS left off, so before you begin work on ISSUES strategies, read, create questions, and share questions about the new story. Use the Reading for Questions and Sharing Questions strategies in any combination that works for you. Then with your interpretive questions and possible answers in hand, you are ready to flesh out your whole issue using the ISSUES strategies.

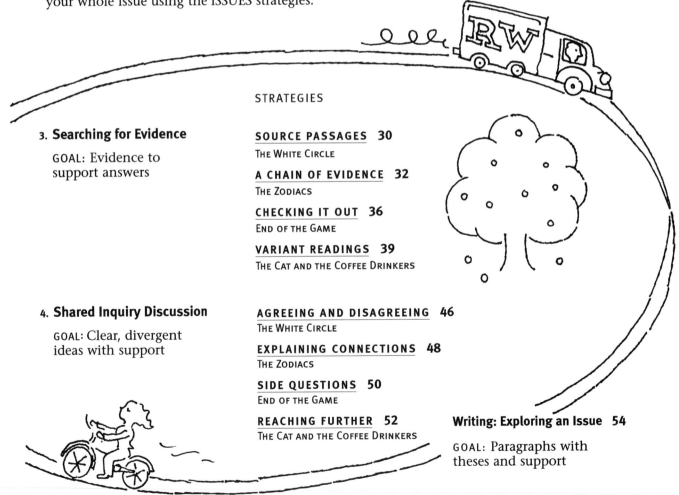

STRATEGIES

3 Searching for Evidence

After your first reading of a story, you had questions and possible answers based on what you read. Now return to the story and seek out whatever relates to your most promising questions.

You'll probably remember many of the details that prompted your questions and answers in the first place, but don't rely on memory alone. When you look through the story a second time, in an organized way, you'll find more details than you can remember, and you'll be able to think them over without guessing about the specifics or getting hung up on the same few ideas.

STARTING POINT

Interpretive Questions

GOAL

Evidence to support answers

Searching for Evidence

Where will you look first for evidence to support your answers? Try the source passage, the part of the story that was the source of your question. Maybe it was a single paragraph, or perhaps a whole scene or incident, that surprised you or stymied you or made you excited or angry. When you explained your question to others, it was a passage you mentioned. When others suggested answers, they looked there to try to back up their ideas.

TO MINE YOUR SOURCE PASSAGE FOR EVIDENCE

* Keep your written question and possible answers close by for reference.

* Skim over what happens in the story before and after your passage to make sure of the context.

* Reread the passage. Include the lead-in sentences and a few sentences after the passage.

* Take notes with your question in mind. Consider what specific words and phrases, actions and descriptions say about your question. (These notes might be quite different from those you took on your first reading.)

* Rewrite your answers—and maybe even your question—based on your notes.

Searching for Evidence

DEMO: SOURCE PASSAGES

One reader wrote this interpretive question after a first reading of "The White Circle":

Does the story want us to think that Tucker is wrong to feel so strongly about his apple tree?

Here is this reader's source passage. Make notes on details that you think might relate to the question.

> Father looked at me for at least a minute. You would have to understand his pride in his colts to understand the way he looked. But at twelve how could I express how *I* felt? My setting such store in having the tree as my own had something to do with the coloring of the apples as they hung among the green leaves; it had something to do with their ripening, not in autumn when the world was full of apples, but in mid-summer when you *wanted* them; but it had more to do with a way of life that had come down through the generations. I would have given one of the apples to Janie. I would have made of it a ceremony. While I would not have said the words, because at twelve you have no such words, I would have handed over the apple with something like this in mind: "Janie, I want to give you this apple. It came from my tree. The tree stands on my father's land. Before my father had the land it belonged to his father, and before that it belonged to my great-grandfather. It's the English family land. It's almost sacred. My possession of this tree forges of me a link in this owning ancestry that must go back clear beyond Moses and all the old Bible folks."

Some of the reader's possible answers are listed below. Do the details you identified support any of these answers?

1. *Yes. Tucker likes to daydream to feel important instead of doing anything practical. He isn't interested in the horse because it requires work.*

2. *No. Tucker is idealistic. He wants to be part of something bigger than himself.*

3. *Yes. Tucker is a snob. He gets his sense of importance from his family rather than his own achievements. He doesn't mind disappointing even his father.*

4. *No. Tucker wants to enjoy his family's way of life. He doesn't realize it is a life of privilege that seems unfair to an outsider like Anvil.*

Now identify a source passage for this question:

Why does Anvil agree to play a little even though he thinks he's getting too old to play?

With a partner, compare the source passages you chose. Why did you pick the passage you chose? Do you agree that the passage your partner picked is a source passage?

Searching for Evidence

STRATEGY: <u>A CHAIN OF EVIDENCE</u>

Often, evidence that relates to your question is scattered throughout the story, in small details that you might have forgotten. Though people talk about "pieces of evidence," separate bits of detail aren't really evidence. A detail in a story becomes evidence only when you connect it with other details, like links in a chain, to support an answer.

Piecing together a chain of evidence from details scattered through a story is like using the Signposts strategy in Reading for Questions, with your questions serving as the signposts:

1. Start by writing down at least two of your interpretive questions, along with their possible answers, so you won't lose focus.

2. Reread the story looking for details that relate to your questions.

3. Think over each detail: How might it connect with each answer? (Many passages will relate to more than one answer—that's why several answers are reasonable.)

4. Be curious and open-minded. Try to link even those details that don't talk directly about your questions to some of your answers.

5. Take notes in your journal or use the organizer on page 35.

6. Bring your notes to discussion so you can easily find your links again.

Searching for Evidence

DEMO: **A CHAIN OF EVIDENCE**

Here is one reader's chain of evidence for a question about "The Zodiacs." Add your own possible answer to the question, then consider which answers the evidence might support.

QUESTION

George at first refused to pay Louie the money he owed and then brought his gang to beat up the team. Later he changed his mind and agreed to pay Louie in order to play for the team for the rest of the season. Why did George change his mind?

POSSIBLE ANSWERS

1. George wants to get fame by playing on the Zodiacs.

2. George tries to look tough, but he's really insecure.

3. George really loves sports, though his brother and his gang don't care about them.

4. _____

EVIDENCE CHAIN

LINK: "Whenever he wanted an audience, George would sit down on the steps of the school . . . and start telling tales of all the jobs he and Vinnie had pulled off" (p. 48).

Supports answer 1. Why? George wants to be well known and his brother's gang helps him achieve it.

Supports answer 2. Why? George has to show off even to younger kids.

LINK: "[Vinnie] was a skinny guy—not at all like George—and the word on him was that he was really chicken. To listen to George, though, you would have thought that Vinnie was the toughest guy ever to hit Brooklyn" (p. 48).

Supports answer 1. Why? George brags about his brother and needs to believe in him because Vinnie is George's greatest claim to fame.

Supports answer____ . Why? _____

_____

_____

LINK: [Louie has the Victrola play "The Star-Spangled Banner."] "I looked at George and he was smiling as broadly as he could, holding his cap across his heart, standing rigid, at attention" (p. 51).

Supports answer _1_. Why? *George could see that Louie was drawing spectators.*

Supports answer_____. Why?_____

_____

_____

Searching for Evidence

A CHAIN OF EVIDENCE ORGANIZER

QUESTION

POSSIBLE ANSWERS

1. _____

2. _____

3. _____

4. _____

EVIDENCE CHAIN

LINK:

Supports answer _____. Why? _____

_____

Supports answer _____. Why? _____

_____

LINK:

Supports answer _____. Why? _____

_____

Supports answer _____. Why? _____

_____

LINK:

Supports answer _____. Why? _____

_____

Supports answer _____. Why? _____

_____

Searching for Evidence

You point to a detail in the story that supports your answer to a question; someone else cites it to support a different idea. Clearly, you can't take some story facts at face value. You need to check them out.

As always, start with a curious attitude. What does this sentence or phrase really mean? How reliable is it? How should you take it? Does the author or character mean it, or is it exaggerated or sarcastic? Ask yourself these questions and jot down a few answers.

Now, track down other aspects of the story that help you resolve your problem details:

1.   Have your interpretive question and answers close at hand.

2.   Focus on evidence that seems related to your question, but is confusing or unclear.

3.   Write queries, things to find out to resolve the confusion.

4.   Working on one query at a time, find passages in the story that help resolve them.

5.   Be demanding. Consider several possible answers to your queries.

6.   Note your new evidence and explanations in your journal.

Searching for Evidence

DEMO: **CHECKING IT OUT**

Here is how one reader began to check out ambiguous evidence from "End of the Game." Add your own evidence to finish the investigation.

Interpretive question: Why does Letitia end the game after Ariel's visit?

Possible answer: Letitia was thrilled when Ariel said in his second note that she was pretty. She was crushed after she realized that Ariel would not continue to think so.

Evidence: Letitia's reaction to Ariel's second note—"But you don't have to exaggerate [your feelings] either, and the way Letitia was acting at the table, or the way she kept the note, was just too much" (p. 69).

Query: Is Letitia exaggerating her feelings or is she really thrilled?

    Possibilities to check out:

1. Not exaggerating. Why is she so excited?

2. Not exaggerating. Why does the narrator say she is?

3. Exaggerating. Why?

Possibility 1. Not exaggerating. Why is she so excited?

Letitia is very happy about being admired by a boy.

    Evidence: She is "the shortest," "very skinny," "scragglier," with "stiffness" in her back that makes her "like a folded-up ironing board" (p. 65). Being considered "the prettiest" is a new experience for her.

Possibility 2. Not exaggerating. Why does the narrator say she is?

a. The narrator is jealous of Letitia.

    Evidence: She and Holanda are "just a little furious" that Ariel prefers Letitia. They all make the statues and attitudes together (p. 68).

    Evidence: _____

_____

_____

b. The narrator speaks impulsively; often says things she doesn't mean.

Evidence: _____

_____

_____

Evidence: _____

_____

_____

Possibility 3. Exaggerating. Why?

Letitia is a very dramatic, imaginative girl; she gets involved with the things she's acting out.

Evidence: Letitia was "the first to start" the game of Statues and Attitudes (p. 64).

Evidence: _____

_____

_____

Searching for Evidence

"Readings" are performances in which literature is read aloud, dramatically. "Readings" can also mean the interpretations different readers may have of a piece of literature. Both kinds of readings are concerned with the same thing—expression.

Readings are "variant" when they vary—when there are several possibilities for what a character or narrator feels or means. Performing variant readings of a source passage will bring out alternative feelings and meanings and help you uncover additional evidence.

1. Team up with one or two partners interested in questions similar to yours.

2. Start with good interpretive questions and answers, written down for easy reference.

3. Decide on a few source passages that you know relate to your questions.

4. Look through each passage for words and phrases that suggest moods or emotions. Is the passage calm, excited, serious, sarcastic, funny?

5. Read your passage aloud to your partners, expressively. Change expression as the incidents and emotions in the passage change.

6. Repeat the process, trying a different set of expressions.

7. Get feedback on each reading from your partners. Which expressions worked? Which didn't?

8. Take notes in your journal so you can refer to them in discussion.

If more than one reading for a single passage worked for you, that means there are different reasonable ways to interpret the passage, and it may be evidence for two or three quite different answers.

Searching for Evidence

DEMO: **VARIANT READINGS**

Here is one reader's interpretive question from "The Cat and the Coffee Drinkers":

Why does Miss Effie say that killing a cat is something she is teaching the children, instead of something that happened accidentally?

Try out variant readings for the reader's source passage on pages 86–87. Begin with "At the end of the first month" and end with "to be drinking it black."

MISS EFFIE: "'Most people spend most of their lives in rooms, and now you know about them.'"	
EXPRESSION: Matter of fact, informative	**BECAUSE:** Miss Effie considers it quite important for children to learn how to behave indoors; she wants the children to understand that it's important.
EXPRESSION: Proud, pleased	**BECAUSE:** Miss Effie wants the children to develop high self-esteem. She says "now you know about them" to make them aware that they know important things.
EXPRESSION:	**BECAUSE:**

NARRATOR: "She then said for the first time a speech which she repeated so often that by the end of the year we sometimes shouted it in our play on the way home."	
EXPRESSION: Amused	**BECAUSE:** The children shout it because they are making fun of Miss Effie.
EXPRESSION: Tolerant	**BECAUSE:** The children shout it because they are proud to be so grown-up.
EXPRESSION:	**BECAUSE:**

MISS EFFIE: "Coffee is a beverage to be enjoyed for its flavor. It is not a food to be enriched with milk and sugar. Only certain types of people try to gain nourishment from it. In general they are the ones, I suspect, who show their emotions in public."	
EXPRESSION: Drily humorous	**BECAUSE:** She knows the children don't understand her.
EXPRESSION:	**BECAUSE:**
EXPRESSION:	**BECAUSE:**

4 Shared Inquiry Discussion

STARTING POINT

Interpretive questions with evidence to support answers

GOAL

Clear, divergent ideas with support

How can you tell when an answer is well supported? What does it sound like? How does it feel? Shared inquiry discussion is an opportunity to find out.

In a good discussion, as you and your classmates propose answers and collect and weigh evidence, you can fully explore the discussion question. Listen for the following:

* Questions, objections, additions to your own answers and evidence

* New answers and evidence that hadn't occurred to you

* Your own second thoughts and inspired ways of saying things

In a shared inquiry discussion, your group can make sense of far more evidence than one person alone could in a week. This team thinking can help you synthesize your answers and evidence into supported ideas. Hone your discussion skills with the Shared Inquiry Discussion strategies on the following pages. Be prepared to change your mind as the group's ideas raise new questions for you.

HOW TO DO SHARED INQUIRY DISCUSSION

* The leader starts discussion with an interpretive question that stirs his or her genuine curiosity. A "further" question from Sharing Questions that has caught both the leader's and the participants' interest might be especially good.

* The leader and participants focus discussion on the story they have all read, rather than other books or personal experiences, so everyone is on equal footing.

* The leader only asks questions, so the participants can take the discussion where they want. Participants can ask questions when they wish.

* The goal of the discussion is for each participant to develop his or her own ideas about the question—not to reach a group consensus or conclusion.

Take a full class period for discussion— 40 minutes at least—so everyone has an opportunity to speak several times. A small group—12 to 18—is most effective.

Building Your Answer with Evidence

After discussion, write a Building Your Answer page for the discussion question as usual, but this time include the evidence for your answer. You'll get good practice at putting this kind of thinking down on paper—practice you'll soon need in writing about your own question.

Discussion question:

_____

_____

_____

My answer before discussion, with evidence to support it:

_____

_____

_____

_____

_____

_____

My answer after discussion, with evidence to support it (add to your original answer or give a new one you heard or thought of in discussion):

_____

_____

_____

_____

_____

_____

_____

Shared Inquiry Discussion

STRATEGY: AGREEING AND DISAGREEING

A powerful way to build thinking in a shared inquiry discussion is for the participants to comment on each other's ideas, agreeing and disagreeing with them. Your goal is to develop each other's ideas as strongly as possible. Responding to each other's ideas is not a debate, a competition, or a negotiation to reach a consensus. (A question to which there is only one answer is hardly a question at all!) Instead, it's a way for everyone to express and explain their own ideas and gain new perspectives from each other. It works in three ways:

* Listening as others comment helps you distinguish their ideas and evidence.

* Getting others' comments on your ideas and evidence helps you strengthen them.

* Commenting on what others say sharpens your ability to work with ideas and gives you new perspectives.

The simplest response is to agree or disagree with someone's statement. The next step is to focus on specific aspects of the statement and to give reasons for your responses. As you think about your response, consider

* What part of the person's comment do you agree with? Disagree with?

* Why do you agree or disagree?

* What evidence do you have?

* What alternative solution to the problem can you offer?

Shared Inquiry Discussion

DEMO: **AGREEING AND DISAGREEING**

Following is a transcript of part of a discussion about "The White Circle." Two participants strongly disagree. As their leader and other participants help them explore the disagreement, their ideas become more interesting and better supported.

LEADER: Whom does the author want us to dislike more, Tucker or Anvil?

DAVID: Anvil, because he's so mean.

AISHA: No, I disagree. Tucker is lots meaner than Anvil.

LEADER: What is especially mean about Tucker or Anvil?

DAVID: The way Anvil pushes Tucker's head into the ground and makes him say all that "Uncle sweetie" stuff.

AISHA: But Tucker wants to do something worse, and he plans to do it. He tries to kill him. Don't you agree that Tucker planned to kill Anvil?

DAVID: Well, yes, but only because Anvil was so mean.

ARLEN: But then why do you think the author wants us to dislike Anvil more if Tucker planned to kill Anvil?

DAVID: Because there's a good reason why Tucker wanted to kill him. But we never understand why Anvil is so mean. He has no reason for it. He seems to enjoy it.

SARA: Aisha, I thought it was very mean when Anvil pushed Tucker's face into the ground. Didn't you think so too?

AISHA: Yes, that was definitely mean. But it was all spur of the moment. He never plotted anything. It wasn't deliberate. It's much uglier to plot and set a trap like Tucker does.

What are some ways to disagree with Aisha?

1. Was it really spur of the moment? He was up in Tucker's tree on purpose.

2. _____

3. _____

What are some ways to disagree with David?

1. You can see from Anvil's father why Anvil was so mean. His father is violent and abusive, and he's made Anvil the same way.

2. _____

3. _____

So which is the story emphasizing more—Tucker's planning or Anvil's being mean for no reason at all?

Shared Inquiry Discussion

Reading means connecting what's on the page with what you know from experience. Common experience is the experience shared by most people. When you state your ideas to others, you'll often make some assumptions about common experience. You'll leave out some connections because you take them for granted. But others who made different connections may be puzzled by yours.

In a shared inquiry discussion, your group can work out these connections for each other:

* Connect an idea or answer with evidence from the story (an incident, a detail, a word or phrase). Try asking

   Where in the story do you see evidence for that?

   Which specific words or phrases in the passage are the relevant ones? Why?

   Is this detail (point it out) also relevant? Why or why not?

* Connect the evidence with common experience to explain what you understand it to mean. Try asking

   What does that mean or show? What is it saying to you?

   Why would a person behave like that? What would cause that?

   What might that word mean in context? Why do you understand it that way?

* Connect your idea of what the evidence means to your interpretive idea or answer. Try asking

   How does that evidence support your answer?

   If that's what's going on, why do you believe _____?

If you get stumped trying to explain your idea

* Explain again, using different words or examples.

* Ask someone who is on your wavelength to help you explain.

If a classmate gets stumped trying to explain, help out:

* If you don't understand, say so in a helpful way.

* Ask about other possible evidence for his or her point.

* Give your own explanation for the evidence and ask what he or she thinks of it.

Don't argue or raise picky objections. The goal is to build everyone's ideas.

Shared Inquiry Discussion

DEMO: **EXPLAINING CONNECTIONS**

Here are some ways students helped two classmates connect their answers to common experience in a discussion of "The Zodiacs."

LEADER: Why did George agree to pay the $8 and come back on the team? *(basic question)*

ANDY: George was an excellent athlete.

KELLI: How do you know from the story that he was an excellent athlete? *(Give evidence from the story.)*

ANDY: It says on page 61 that as a sophomore he was starting pitcher for his high school team.

BRYCE: How does that show he was an excellent athlete? *(Connect the evidence with common experience.)*

ANDY: Sophomores are the second-youngest students in high school. Starting pitcher is the most demanding position on a baseball team. If George was starting pitcher when he was a sophomore, he must have been very good.

KELLI: How does that explain why he was willing to pay the $8? *(Connect the evidence with the original question.)*

ANDY: People usually like to do things they are very good at doing. He probably really liked to play baseball, maybe more than hanging out with Vinnie's gang.

LEADER: Connor, why do you think George agreed to pay the $8 and come back on the team? *(basic question again)*

CONNOR: George's other choices were closed off by the fight.

ANTHONY: How did the fight close off choices? *(Support the fact from the story.)*

CONNOR: The police told the Zodiacs and George's gang after the fight that Vinnie was a coward. That's page 60. The Zodiacs will be able to tell everybody at school the truth. Now they'll all know.

SCOTT: Why would that be important to George? *(Connect the evidence with common experience.)*

CONNOR: George was a bragger. People who brag are usually trying to feel important. If they can't feel important one way, they will try to find another way to get attention.

STACY: How do you know George bragged? *(Give evidence from the story.)*

CONNOR: On page 48, it says George bragged about Vinnie to all the kids.

TIARA: If he can't brag about Vinnie anymore, why will that make him pay the $8 to go back to the Zodiacs? *(Connect the evidence with the original question.)*

CONNOR: Because winning all those games, getting his name in the paper—the things he did with the Zodiacs—give him another way to be important and have things to brag about. Even if it's humiliating to pay the money, it's still worth it.

Shared Inquiry Discussion

Often in discussion, someone's answer will open up one particular facet of the basic question—a side question. You can learn a lot by focusing on the side question for a while before returning to the main question. In fact, pursuing several side questions, one at a time, helps you dig deeper into different aspects of your basic question.

Like all open, interpretive questions, side questions are based on curiosity, surprise, or puzzlement.

HERE ARE SOME SURPRISES THAT MIGHT PROMPT USEFUL SIDE QUESTIONS:

* As a person explains an answer, he or she seems to contradict the original statement.

* As a person explains an answer, you move from agreeing to disagreeing with it.

* Two other people disagree or agree unexpectedly.

* An answer seems odd, surprising, or inconsistent with the way you think things usually happen.

WHEN ASKING SIDE QUESTIONS

* Let curiosity be your guide; be sensitive to surprises and seeming contradictions.

* Give everyone a chance to answer the side question, though not everyone will want to.

* If no one answers, explain where you "got" the side question. Still no interest? Move on.

Since a side question starts with an answer to the basic question, it should connect back to that question. As people develop answers to the side question, ask them to explain how they relate to the basic question.

Shared Inquiry Discussion

DEMO: **SIDE QUESTIONS**

Is it a side question or the same question put in a different way?

> Side question—focuses on one specific aspect of the basic question
> Same question—does not add focus

Is it a side question or a tangent?

> Side question—ties back to the basic question
> Tangent—leads away from the basic question

Test the following questions with possible answers and try to tie them back to the basic question, Why do they stop playing the game after Ariel's visit?

> Why doesn't Letitia want to play the game any more?
> What was the point of the game?
> Why does Ariel sit on the other side of the train after Letitia's last statue?
> Why does Letitia want to make one more statue before ending the game?

The following transcript shows how some side questions came up during a discussion. What side questions would you have asked? Why?

LEADER: Why do they stop playing the game after Ariel's visit? *(basic question)*

RAYMOND: I think Letitia is the leader of it all. *(Give evidence and explanation.)*

LEADER: If Letitia was the leader of it all, why did the younger girls play the game?

RAYMOND: The younger girls got caught up in the imagination of the game. *(Explain evidence.)*

LEON: Well, so then why did the younger girls stop playing the game when Letitia stopped? *(Side question: Try to tie Raymond's answer back to the basic question.)*

RAYMOND: The younger girls were in awe of her. She was by far the most imaginative of them.

LEADER: Andrea, why do you think they stopped playing the game after Ariel's visit? *(basic question again)*

ANDREA: When Ariel said he would come, Letitia was very upset because she didn't want him to know she was handicapped, not beautiful. So then Letitia felt that the game had been a lie. She wrote Ariel the truth in her letter, and she stopped the game. *(Give evidence and explanation.)*

LEADER: Do you think Letitia considered the game itself deceptive? *(Side question: Try to see whether other participants agree or disagree with this idea.)*

CHANTAL: I think they all did, after they saw how Ariel got the wrong idea.

LEADER: Why would being deceptive make them stop the game, when they are deceiving their parents to play the game in the first place? *(Side question: Try to tie Chantal's question back to the basic question.)*

Shared Inquiry Discussion

STRATEGY: **REACHING FURTHER**

Your shared inquiry discussion has warmed up, and there are strong ideas out on the table. People are speaking energetically, with feeling. Now, pull back from the discussion for a moment and ask yourself, Where is this discussion going? What question are people really answering? Are we still on the original question?

Often, one of two things is happening:

1. People are working on questions about their own experience or other knowledge, not the story everyone has shared. You would need some research before you could support your ideas with strong evidence. Ask yourself

   Does the story present it that way, or is that the way you see it?
   Is this idea in the story or in your head?

2. The focus is still on the story, but the comments reach further, pointing to a larger, deeper question in it. Ask yourself

   Is this what the basic question is really asking, or is it a different problem?
   Is this a more powerful version of the basic question or a watered down one?
   Are we really digging now, or are we shooting the breeze?

Try to reach for that further question and express it to the group. Ask them

   "Is the story really saying _____?"

   "Are we supposed to believe or feel that _____?"

Shared Inquiry Discussion

DEMO: **REACHING FURTHER**

Consider each of the questions following one leader's basic question for "The Cat and the Coffee Drinkers." Does it extend the question or not?

BASIC QUESTION: Why does Miss Effie say that killing a cat was something she was teaching the children?

Was my kindergarten teacher nicer than Miss Effie?

What are we meant to think the children learned from killing the cat?

Why does the narrator say that Miss Effie "had nothing more to teach us" after killing the cat?

Did you have experiences with the death of a pet when you were a child?

What should children learn in kindergarten?

Why does Miss Effie have no sympathy, apparently, for the cat or for the children?

Should people humanely kill animals that are suffering hopelessly?

Does the story present killing the cat as a new lesson for the children, or a continuation of Miss Effie's earlier teaching?

Writing: Exploring an Issue

STARTING POINT

Interpretive questions with evidence to support answers; answers and evidence explained

GOAL

Paragraphs with theses and support

ASSIGNMENT

In a short essay, introduce and explain one of your questions and then explain at least two possible answers to it, showing how they are supported with evidence from the text.

AUDIENCE

Students who have read the story but have not thought very deeply about it and do not necessarily share your ideas about it.

PURPOSE

To interest your readers in what you consider an exciting aspect of the story. The more distinct and well supported your possible answers, the more engaged your readers are likely to be.

FORMAT

In two to three typed, double-spaced pages

* Introduce and explain your question (one paragraph)

* Explain several possible answers (one or two paragraphs for each answer)

  Each paragraph should have a thesis statement—an answer to the question—with explanation and evidence to support the thesis.

* Conclude by weighing the evidence and deciding on a best answer *or* by proposing and explaining a further question (one paragraph).

SHOW YOUR WORK

Along with your essay, turn in

* Your initial questions

* Your notes, organizers, and drafts

For more guidance see the grading rubric on the facing page (p. 55) and the sample student papers for Exploring an Issue (pp. 105–116).

CONVENTIONS TO MASTER

* Directly quoting words, phrases, and pieces of dialogue from the story

* Referencing or footnoting page numbers for quoted and paraphrased passages

* Drawing a conclusion for each paragraph with a sentence linking the evidence back to your question

Writing: Exploring an Issue

CONTENT

EXPERT (5) The essay gives the reader a fresh and interesting insight into the story.

* The topic question is significant, intriguing, and immediately opens up ideas about the story.

* The paragraph theses give a variety of distinct perspectives on the story that are strongly supported with evidence from the story.

PRACTITIONER (3) The essay gives the reader a competent view of the story.

* The topic question focuses on the story and is fairly clear and interesting.

* The paragraph theses suggest a few different ideas about the story that have some evidence from the story to back them up.

BEGINNER (1) The essay gives the reader some references to the story.

* The question is confusing or vague, could apply to any story, or is otherwise lacking.

* The paragraph theses are all versions of the same idea, or are far-fetched or obvious, and are supported only with very sparse or vague evidence from the story.

ORGANIZATION

EXPERT (5) The essay explores the topic question in an orderly way, with each part of the essay making its own contribution to the exploration.

* The introduction clearly states and explains the topic question.

* Paragraph theses are distinct, each responding to the topic question.

* Each paragraph presents and explains evidence from the story that supports its thesis strongly.

PRACTITIONER (3) The essay remains focused on the topic question, but there are gaps and repetition in the exploration of it.

* The introduction states the topic question and may restate it.

* Paragraph theses mostly differ from each other and respond to the topic question.

* Each paragraph cites evidence from the story and relates it loosely to its thesis.

BEGINNER (1) The essay seems to loose track of the topic question, leaving ideas incomplete and repeating ideas.

* The introduction is lacking, or the statement of the topic question is unclear or confusing.

* Paragraph theses are lacking, overly simple, or repeat or overlap each other.

* Some paragraphs lack support for theses.

VOICE

EXPERT (5) The essay strongly engages the reader with the sense of an individual writer who has thought energetically about the story. The writer seems to offer ideas with sincere interest.

PRACTITIONER (3) The essay gives the sense of a pleasant, well-intentioned writer who has given some thought to the story. The writer seems to offer ideas in an "all in a day's work" way.

BEGINNER (1) The essay gives little sense of an individual writer's thinking behind it. The writer seems to be indifferent or going through the motions.

WORD CHOICE

Apply your usual standards for word choice.

SENTENCE FLUENCY

Apply your usual standards for sentence fluency.

CONVENTIONS

Apply your usual standards for conventions.

PROCESS OF THINKING AND WRITING

EXPERT (5) Complete notes show the growth of possible answers and the development of evidence to support them.

PRACTITIONER (3) Competent notes show choice among possible answers and possible evidence.

BEGINNER (1) Very sparse notes, or none; no process of growth can be traced.

Writing: Exploring an Issue

STRATEGY: **YOU AND YOUR READERS**

Think of your audience, the people who will read your essay. For this essay, it's probably someone who has read the story but doesn't necessarily share your views about it. Your most likely readers are your classmates, including good friends, sworn enemies, and everyone in between.

Although, as people, your readers are very different from you and from each other, as readers, you and they probably share certain likes and dislikes. So what do you like to read?

I WOULD RATHER READ

❏ An assertive statement that I might disagree with

❏ A bland, cautious statement that anyone would agree with

❏ A lengthy rehash of story facts that I already know

❏ A quick reminder of story facts that I already know

❏ An argument that spells out one side of the question as if it's the only answer

❏ An argument that takes other ideas into account

❏ A train of thought that I have to piece together myself

❏ A train of thought that the writer links together clearly

❏ Writing with a down-to-earth, confident tone that is a little messy

❏ Writing with an elaborate, "put on" style that is very correct

The Golden Rule: Do unto your readers as you would have writers do unto you.

Writing: Exploring an Issue

STRATEGY: **STRONG FOUNDATIONS**

One key to good writing is putting your effort where it will pay off most. Your whole essay depends on a strong question (the topic of your essay) and strong answers (the theses of your paragraphs). Strengthen these parts before you draft the whole essay.

In discussion, you strengthen your ideas when other people talk back to you, questioning you and offering their alternative views. Keep the momentum from discussion by talking through your question with a partner or a small group—or "talk back" to yourself.

Ask the kinds of questions you used in Sharing Questions and in Shared Inquiry Discussion. Imagine how another person might understand—or misunderstand—your ideas. Work "talking back" into each step of planning your essay:

1. Write your question at the top of the page.

2. Draft your answers in one sentence each. Leave lots of space between them.

3. Under each answer, briefly note the evidence you will include for it.

4. Talk back to each answer and its evidence, jotting down notes of new evidence and explanations to add.

5. Rewrite each answer as an entirely new sentence.

6. Look over your "new" answers and rewrite your question based on them.

Now you're ready to draft a stronger, more thought-through essay.

Writing: Exploring an Issue

DEMO: **STRONG FOUNDATIONS**

Here is one writer's foundation for "The Zodiacs." This writer revised the question twice and each answer once, dropping and adding some evidence.

Question

~~Why is George able to ruin Louie's plan?~~

~~Was it a foolish plan to begin with?~~

Does the story show that Louie's plan was too ~~optimistic~~ ambitious from the start?

  Explain: "plan" = make the team famous as a great team

Thesis 1

~~Yes. Louie's plan depended on George, and Louie couldn't handle George.~~

Yes. Louie underestimated how much George needed to be the tough guy and not let anyone boss him around.

Evidence:

 All the kids were afraid when Louie suggests having George

 Louie insisted he could handle George

  Explain: Louie more naïve than the others

 George doesn't come to practice—Louie doesn't try to make him

 ~~Louie gives suggestions on plays~~

 George disrespects the team and Louie

  Explain: George has a different attitude toward Louie than toward the rest of the boys?

Evidence for revised thesis:

 George admires and wants to imitate his brother

 George could not get the lottery money from his brother's gang

Thesis 2

~~No. The plan was a success; the Zodiacs got to be far more famous than a kid's team would.~~

No. The original plan was successful as long as Louie focused on baseball.

Evidence:

Louie knew the pitcher was the key; they won every game

Louie did get George to play

Louie scouted the Raiders—had a strategy

Louie attracted attention—"Star-Spangled Banner"

Louie got article in the paper

~~George's gang helped raise money~~

Explain: George did respect Louie up to a point

Evidence for revised thesis:

Uniforms were to help the team live up to their name

Selling lottery tickets involved George in something besides baseball

Explain: looking good instead of winning baseball—Was Louie's ego involved?

Conclusion

Ego always a danger for Louie as well as George

Writing: Exploring an Issue

STRONG FOUNDATIONS ORGANIZER #1

The model below shows how your question, with answers and evidence, should hang together.

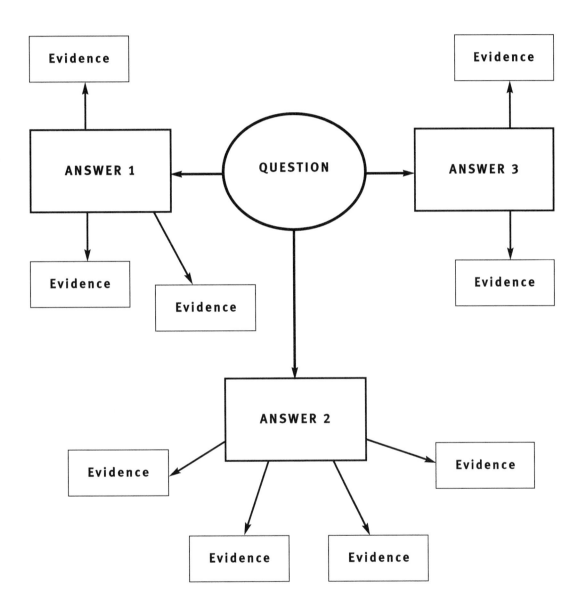

Positions

By this time you're eager to take a stand on your favorite question. The possible answers you've considered and the evidence you've explored have convinced you of the best answer to your question. This is your position, and you're ready to share it with a wider audience.

But are you ready to write? You want others to adopt, or at least respect, your position. Are you ready to re-create your thinking fully enough, and convincingly enough, that others will join you?

Even if you are a hyper-organized note-taker with no doodles in your journal, your ideas are probably still all over the place. When thinking or talking about them, you jump easily from one idea to another as they swirl freely through your mind. But an essay has to have a starting point, and it has to advance step by step. That's why most of us hesitate before we begin writing. We've all started writing essays and found that some ideas evaporated, or that there seemed to be no room for others. In POSITIONS, you'll extend your ideas and organize them into a working outline. Then you'll be able to write a substantial essay over several writing sessions and include all of your thinking.

POSITIONS is based on your work from QUESTIONS and ISSUES. If you're working on a new story, start the process from the beginning, reading and creating questions, searching for evidence, and participating in shared inquiry discussion, using the strategies that work best for you. Then take on POSITIONS.

Shared Inquiry Discussion

Explaining and supporting your ideas in discussion are becoming habits. What more do you need to strengthen your own position? You need to know other people's positions on the story. This may sound contradictory, but it isn't. To put your idea across, you have to be ready to counter opposing ideas that others in your group may have and answer their objections. Discussion is a great opportunity to do this. Agree and disagree, explaining your opinions. Ask side questions and further questions about ideas that interest you or that you may want to challenge.

> **STARTING POINT**
> Interpretive questions with evidence to support answers

> **GOAL**
> Clear, divergent ideas with support explained

Now, supplement your group's discussion by conducting your own mini-discussions with classmates who are working on questions related to yours. Have each member of the group lead a brief discussion about his or her own question. The shared inquiry strategies in ISSUES can help you lead effectively. Make up for your group's small size by deliberately bringing up diverse opinions. Above all, keep it experimental and open-minded; don't decide too soon what your position will be.

HOW TO DO SHARED INQUIRY DISCUSSION

* The leader starts discussion with an interpretive question that stirs his or her genuine curiosity. A "further" question from Sharing Questions that has caught both the leader's and the participants' interest might be especially good.

* The leader and participants focus discussion on the story they have all read, rather than other books or personal experiences, so everyone is on equal footing.

* The leader only asks questions, so the participants can take the discussion where they want. Participants can ask questions when they wish.

* The goal of the discussion is for each participant to develop his or her own ideas about the question—not to reach a group consensus or conclusion.

Take a full class period for discussion—40 minutes at least—so everyone has an opportunity to speak several times. A small group—12 to 18—is most effective.

5 Crafting a Position

In your journal, write down all of your ideas about your basic question—just a few words to remind you of each. Don't try to put them in order, just scatter them about the page as they come to you. Talk them over with someone else. Track down more evidence as you need it to respond to what other people think. Write down this new evidence, too. *Writing is vital;* it gets your thoughts out there where you can work with them methodically, so they're not swirling around in your head anymore.

STARTING POINT

Interpretive questions; clear, divergent ideas with support explained

GOAL

Extended ideas and support

Home in on the ideas you find most convincing. Consider how you will explain and support them and relate them to each other. Work also with the ideas that don't persuade you, but that do persuade other people. To convince them, you will have to show that these ideas are included in yours or that they are not as well supported and sensible as yours.

Crafting a Position

In shared inquiry discussion, you and your classmates have developed a good question into an issue with many well-supported possible answers. Now map it all out on paper. You'll be able to see which answers and support feed into your position and which you must reply to or argue with.

TO MAP AN ISSUE

* Get the whole discussion group to work on the map soon after discussion, so ideas don't evaporate.

* Lay out on paper or a blackboard the discussion question and the major side questions.

* Fill in the answers you heard for them and note briefly the support for each.

* Consider how answers relate to each other; draw arrows or write notes to show connections.

* Talk through the answers, jotting down enough details—quotes, page numbers, catch words—so that you all can reconstruct the support and explanation in your heads.

Crafting a Position

DEMO: **MAPPING, PART 1**

Which parts of the issue from "The Diary of a Young Girl" mapped below would you include in your position? How would you strengthen your position?

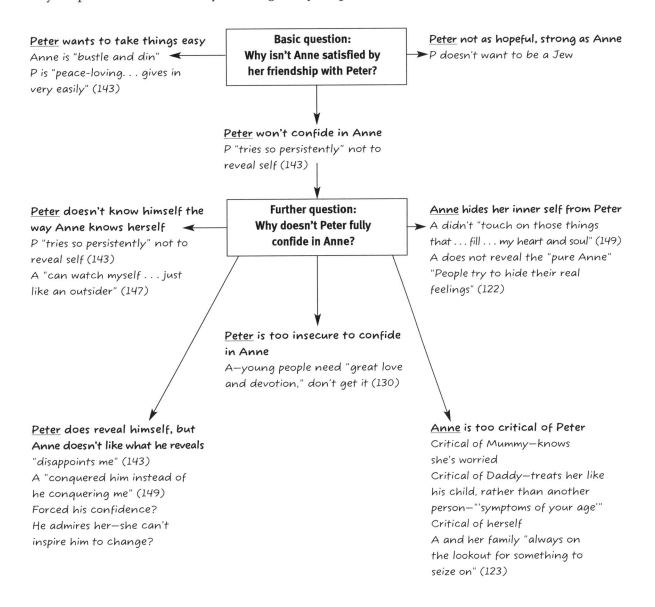

Peter wants to take things easy
Anne is "bustle and din"
P is "peace-loving. . . gives in
very easily" (143)

Basic question:
Why isn't Anne satisfied by
her friendship with Peter?

Peter not as hopeful, strong as Anne
P doesn't want to be a Jew

Peter won't confide in Anne
P "tries so persistently" not to
reveal self (143)

Peter doesn't know himself the
way Anne knows herself
P "tries so persistently" not to
reveal self (143)
A "can watch myself . . . just
like an outsider" (147)

Further question:
Why doesn't Peter fully
confide in Anne?

Anne hides her inner self from Peter
A didn't "touch on those things
that . . . fill . . . my heart and soul" (149)
A does not reveal the "pure Anne"
"People try to hide their real
feelings" (122)

Peter is too insecure to confide
in Anne
A—young people need "great love
and devotion," don't get it (130)

Peter does reveal himself, but
Anne doesn't like what he reveals
"disappoints me" (143)
A "conquered him instead of
he conquering me" (149)
Forced his confidence?
He admires her—she can't
inspire him to change?

Anne is too critical of Peter
Critical of Mummy—knows
she's worried
Critical of Daddy—treats her like
his child, rather than another
person—"'symptoms of your age'"
Critical of herself
A and her family "always on
the lookout for something to
seize on" (123)

Crafting a Position

Have you outgrown your original question? It would be surprising if you had not. Your answers and evidence have grown; so you probably need a question of greater breadth and depth. Time to rework your original question into a further question that can launch you to a stronger position.

You have considered further questions as they arose naturally in shared inquiry. Now dig for them by talking over your entire issue with a partner (or with yourself, if you can be hard on yourself). Use these question stems to help you:

* Is the story really saying that _____?

* Are we supposed to believe or feel that _____?

* Is the author's idea that _____?

* Is this [character or incident] supposed to be unusual, more _____ than usual?

* Is this [character or incident] supposed to be the way life usually is, because _____?

Look for a further question that ties together all your ideas, or that expresses what is most interesting about them.

As you work with a partner or by yourself, take notes! Even when your ideas are not there yet, note possibilities to build on later.

Crafting a Position

DEMO: USING FURTHER QUESTIONS, PART 1

Below is a conference in which one writer and a partner used further questions to develop an issue from "The Secret Lion."

BASIC QUESTION: Why did the boys bury the grinding ball?

IDEAS: The boys buried the grinding ball so it wouldn't be treated as ordinary junk. Their mothers would tell them to throw out the things they found. It seemed that their mothers were keeping them from the important things, like going to the arroyo or the hills. Now they want to keep something important—the grinding ball—to themselves. They don't have a place to do that, so they bury it.

PARTNER: Why is making that change a big deal in the story?

WRITER: They've always been pretty independent, trying to discover things for themselves. That's what they mainly do in the story. They go to the arroyo and the hills.

PARTNER: Their being independent, going to these places—what does that have to do with the ball?

WRITER: [gives up] Well, I guess it's really kind of stupid.

PARTNER: [keeps working] No, you were interested in that. Going to the places—what is there about that?

WRITER: [takes a useful detour] I think a lot of kids want to go off on their own. We never could much in our neighborhood, but it's exciting to go away, to be on your own, when you're a kid.

PARTNER: [asks a further question] So is that your opinion or the author's? Does he think being on your own is such a big step? Or just the boys—?

WRITER: [thinks out loud] It seems like, for him, that's what growing up is about. You don't get things really, he says, "things get taken away," but you have the experience of trying things out.

PARTNER: [asks another further question] So we're supposed to get that they're learning—

WRITER: They aren't learning what they want to learn. Not in school. They're just shouting it to each other. Just to experience it.

PARTNER: Experiencing. The author wants to show experiencing? Now with the ball, losing it by burying it, what kind of experience—

WRITER: [thinks out loud] Okay, well, they are growing up. And now they've decided they will be in control. They will take care of the ball, or they'll let it get taken away themselves. Not someone like the golfers or their mothers throwing it out. It will be their choice. And they won't try to hold on to it.

PARTNER: So the point is control?

WRITER: No, wait; the point is experience. If it's in your experience, you want to be in control of it. Not let it get taken over by someone else at the end. The big point is experience. First they choose to go off on their own to the interesting places, whether they are forbidden or not. Then they try things out there, having their own Coke holder, shouting dirty words, admiring the grinding ball. Then they make the move to take control of the experience so they have it, even if other people want to take it away.

PARTNER: OK, so experience. So your question is not just why did they bury it, but why does that, how does that relate to their own experience?

WRITER: Yeah. Why do they have to bury it to have it be an experience? Or, why do they have to make sure the grinding ball isn't taken away? Why does burying it preserve their experience of finding it?

PARTNER: Write that down!

Crafting a Position

Try thinking about your issue as a tree, with your basic question and answer as the trunk. Like a tree, your issue has roots that feed into the trunk:

* Initial questions that led you to your basic question

* Source passages

* Possible answers and supporting evidence

* Ideas you said or heard in discussion

Your issue also has branches and twigs—questions and ideas that extend your issue further and help you see more in the story. Look for

* Additional passages where you might see your issue

* Reasons for or explanations of incidents or characters

* Questions you still have

* Alternatives or contradictions to your issue

Crafting a Position

DEMO: **AN ISSUE TREE, PART 1**

Below is one writer's issue tree for "Day of the Butterfly." Consider the roots and branches and add your own twigs.

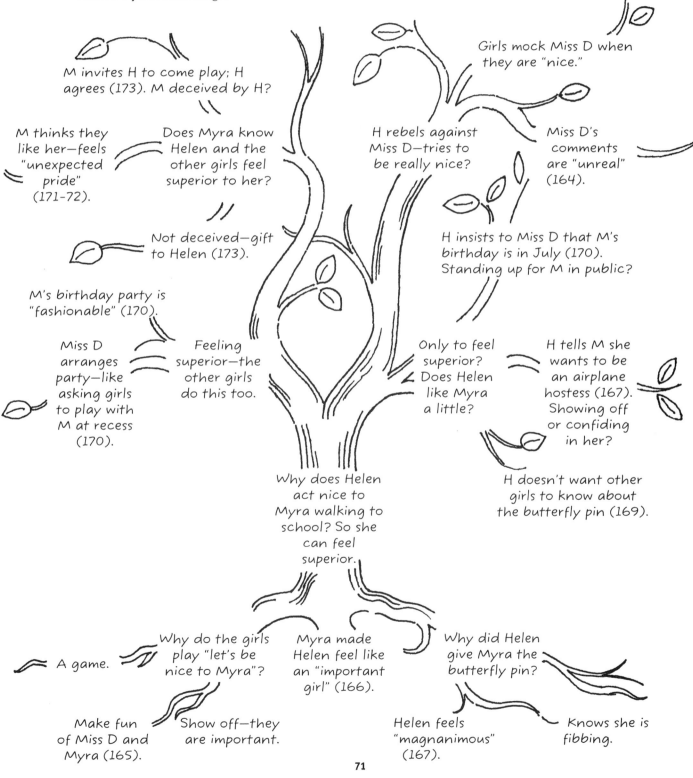

M invites H to come play; H agrees (173). M deceived by H?

M thinks they like her—feels "unexpected pride" (171-72).

Does Myra know Helen and the other girls feel superior to her?

Not deceived—gift to Helen (173).

Girls mock Miss D when they are "nice."

H rebels against Miss D—tries to be really nice?

Miss D's comments are "unreal" (164).

H insists to Miss D that M's birthday is in July (170). Standing up for M in public?

M's birthday party is "fashionable" (170).

Miss D arranges party—like asking girls to play with M at recess (170).

Feeling superior—the other girls do this too.

Only to feel superior? Does Helen like Myra a little?

H tells M she wants to be an airplane hostess (167). Showing off or confiding in her?

H doesn't want other girls to know about the butterfly pin (169).

Why does Helen act nice to Myra walking to school? So she can feel superior.

A game.

Why do the girls play "let's be nice to Myra"?

Myra made Helen feel like an "important girl" (166).

Why did Helen give Myra the butterfly pin?

Make fun of Miss D and Myra (165).

Show off—they are important.

Helen feels "magnanimous" (167).

Knows she is fibbing.

Crafting a Position

If you've got lots of questions and ideas but are having trouble sorting them out, clustering will help you organize them into a solid position. To form clusters

* Write each of your questions and possible answers on a notecard or slip of paper.

* Sort the notecards into clusters of ideas that seem related. (If a card fits into more than one cluster, make duplicate cards and include one in each cluster.)

* Find—or write—the basic idea or question that all the ideas in the cluster seem to point to. To test your basic question, ask: Do all the other questions and ideas in the cluster help to answer it? Does it seem very important to the meaning of the story?

* Now choose your favorite cluster. Add questions that fill in any gaps by bringing up different aspects of the question and alternative ideas that should be addressed. Weed out any questions in the cluster that repeat other questions or move away from your basic question. Test each question in the cluster by asking: Will answering this question help me answer my basic question?

* Now note the answers to your new questions, as well as evidence to support them.

You should end up with your "old" ideas logically arranged, plus many new ideas.

Crafting a Position

DEMO: <u>CLUSTERING QUESTIONS AND IDEAS, PART 1</u>

Here are the clusters two writers made for *A Christmas Carol,* with the questions and ideas they added or rewrote and those they crossed out. Add or rewrite two cluster ideas or questions for each cluster.

Cluster 1

~~Basic question: Scrooge already decided to reform before the Ghost of the Future comes. Why does he have to have that ghost?~~

Basic question: The Ghost of Christmas Yet to Come shows Scrooge only horrible or sad things. Why doesn't the ghost show him how good it would be to reform?

> Scrooge has to see where his selfish life is leading him. He has to think the future is all decided unless he does something to change it.

Why does Scrooge have to see Tiny Tim's death, too?

> Compare Scrooge with Tiny Tim. Anyone would be sorrier about Tiny Tim's death than Scrooge's—even Scrooge is.

> Scrooge is responsible for Tiny Tim as well as for himself, because if Scrooge learns to be generous to Bob Cratchit, he can save Tiny Tim's life.

> Tiny Tim's death and the memory of him will help the Cratchits live better lives; Scrooge's death gives the people who work for him the opportunity to make themselves worse by stealing from his body.

Why doesn't Scrooge guess that he is the dead person?

Does Scrooge's pleading change the ghost's mind about whether his future is already decided?

Why do the other ghosts also show Scrooge upsetting things?

Why does the Ghost of Christmas Past show Scrooge his fiancée and her husband pitying his loneliness? Why does that upset him so much, when it was partly his decision not to marry?

Why does the Ghost of Christmas Present show Scrooge Ignorance and Want after showing him all the happy Christmases people are celebrating?

Cluster 2

Basic idea: Christmas makes it possible for Scrooge to reform because everyone is kind and generous then.

ADD: and because Christmas includes both being kind to others and enjoying good things for yourself.

Scrooge is really happy when he wakes up and finds out it's still Christmas. ~~Why does it matter so much if he plans to reform?~~

ADD: He might feel that Christmas is the best time to start leading his new life.

It seems really easy for Scrooge to reform. As soon as he wakes up, he begins, and he knows exactly what to do.

Why is Scrooge so eager to join in the fun at his nephew's? It's catching.

Did Marley's ghost get to appear to Scrooge because it was Christmas?

Scrooge is so mean because he had only a few happy times in his early life. The Ghost of Christmas Past shows him how lonely his childhood was.

Why doesn't the Ghost of Christmas Present show Scrooge Want and Ignorance until he asks?

Does Scrooge learn from his nephew's comments that he feels sorry for Scrooge?

Scrooge is not bothered by them. Not really true.

Nephew is proving that he isn't being nice to Scrooge just to get his money. Note: Scrooge never accuses him of this.

ADD: The Cratchits are very poor, but they are happy. Why doesn't the Ghost of Christmas Present show Scrooge people who are miserable and need help?

The ghost wants to show the joy of Christmas. Be generous because you feel joy, not vice versa.

ADD: Seeing Old Fezziwig again makes Scrooge start wanting to be kind to Bob Cratchit, even before he knows about Tiny Tim.

ADD: When he sees his schoolmates, he wishes he had given the carol singer something.

6 Nailing It Down

Now nail down those free-floating ideas into a plan or an outline for an essay—everything you want to include in the order you want it:

1. An introduction presenting your question in a way that will intrigue your reader. A forceful statement of your question and your position might be your best opening! Other possibilities include

   * Why your question is interesting or important to you

   * An example of your position from real life

   * An opposing position that your essay will argue against

2. An essay thesis—a sentence stating your position. Since this thesis will be the heart of a substantial essay, more than ever it should be

   * Clear and distinctive in meaning

   * Assertive—people can agree or disagree with it

   * Significant—it can change a person's whole idea of the story

3. Ideas that explain and support your essay thesis. Present each idea in a separate paragraph. For each paragraph, include

   * A transitional word or phrase in the first sentence to connect the paragraph with the one preceding it

   * A thesis stating the main idea for the paragraph

   * Explanation and evidence to clarify and support the idea

   * A conclusion that sums up the idea and relates it to the essay question

4. A conclusion tying it all together. The conclusion should give the reader a final statement. It might also include

   * How you would apply your position to your own life

   * A further insight into the story you gained in presenting your position

   * A question that you are left with after presenting your position

When you sit down to write your essay, you might prefer to write the first paragraph last, after you've written out all of your ideas and support.

Nailing It Down

STRATEGY: **MAPPING, PART 2**

The map you created in Crafting a Position on page 66 shows a whole issue as you and your classmates explored it in discussion. You can also map your own position to see how your ideas are related to each other.

TRY OUT SEVERAL ARRANGEMENTS FOR YOUR IDEAS:

1. Write each idea on a single notecard. Add your best evidence for it.

2. For each idea you disagree with, write your response and reasons on the notecard.

3. Lay out the notecards to create a map with related ideas near each other.

4. Is it clear how your ideas are related? Jot down a few notes to remind you of the connections you see.

5. Add new ideas on separate notecards if you see gaps in your map.

THEN, MOVE FROM THE MAP TO AN OUTLINE:

1. Rewrite your basic question into a strong thesis statement that sums up your position on the whole issue.

2. Arrange your notecards—with their added notes—in a logical order so that each leads to the next.

3. Emphasize the most important points by putting them first and last.

4. When you find the arrangement that seems best, tape your cards down onto a large sheet of paper or onto your desk. Deal with them one by one as you write.

Is this method new to you? If so, get together with one or two partners who have issues related to yours. Write up your notecards separately, then talk through together ways to map each other's ideas.

Nailing It Down

DEMO: **MAPPING, PART 2**

Below is one writer's outline based on the map of an issue from "The Diary of a Young Girl" on page 71. One idea became the thesis for the outline; others became points supporting the thesis. Also, some new ideas (underlined) came to the writer while creating the outline. Still another idea from the map inspired a conclusion.

Intro (hook): Love—the more Peter needs it, the harder it is for him to get.

~~*Thesis: Anne is disappointed in her relationship with Peter because he does not confide in her the way she wants him to.*~~

Thesis: Peter and Anne are both disappointed in their relationship because Peter is too insecure to confide in Anne.

Point 1: Peter doesn't confide

  He "tries so persistently" to hide his feelings

  Hints of how he wants to confide in Anne—Find new support!

  Anne feels that he never does confide in her

Point 2: Why Peter hides his feelings—insecure

  Young people need "great love and devotion"—Peter doesn't get that from his parents

  Mother's criticisms

  Father?

Upset about hiding

  Doesn't want to be a Jew

  Knows that Anne criticizes some of his feelings, his family

  Disagree that Peter is easygoing, peaceloving—that is just the way he looks to others

  Anne also hides inner self; looks like a "little goat"

Point 3: Anne much more hopeful and confident than Peter

  She doesn't sympathize with his fears

  When Peter does reveal things, Anne doesn't approve of them

Conclusion: Peter hides his feelings, but he is really no different from anyone else

  Anne says people hide their true selves from others

Nailing It Down

Often, the sentence or two you stammer out in response to further questions summarizes your position very well! When this happens, you have a ready-made thesis for your essay. Once you have it, check to make sure it pulls in all the aspects that you feel strongly about:

* List the points you made and work with them one at a time.

* Explain to yourself or a partner how they fit your thesis.

* If one of your points doesn't fit with your thesis, try to rewrite your thesis to pull it in.

* Use this thesis and list of points as a rough outline for your essay, where each point will be the thesis of a paragraph.

Nailing It Down

DEMO: **USING FURTHER QUESTIONS, PART 2**

The writer in the "The Secret Lion" conference on page 69 drafted the thesis and list of points below. Can you locate where the main points and support came up in the writer's work on finding a further question?

Thesis: In this story, the experience of being independent is what really matters in growing up.

> Example of acting independent: Burying the grinding ball instead of trying to keep it

Independent experience 1: They know and expect that things will get taken away

> Places like the golf course aren't really theirs

> Arroyo—their place—is a mess with sewage

Independent experience 2: They make the choice

> Take it home—mothers throw it out

> Lose it themselves—don't have it taken away

Independent experience 3: Appreciate the experience of having it

> Shout things to each other in the arroyo—solve high school problems

> Don't look hard for grinding ball—already appreciated the experience of it

Conclusion: Even if opportunities are limited—"things get taken away"—growing up can feel worthwhile.

Nailing It Down

The roots of your issue tree can make a good introduction for your thesis. Sharing with your readers where and how you first got interested in your position can help them get interested in it, too.

WHEN WRITING AN INTRODUCTION BASED ON "ROOT" IDEAS

* Summarize the part of the story that sparked your original question to remind the reader of it.

* Explain why you are interested in your question.

* Be dramatic!

* Give an example of your position from real life.

* Keep your introduction brief. Lead directly into your thesis.

Nailing It Down

DEMO: **AN ISSUE TREE, PART 2**

The writer of the issue tree on page 71 used one of the roots to make this dramatic introduction to her essay:

> When is it not nice to be nice to someone? When it's a game! A group of girls on the playground say, "Let's be nice to Myra!" and go say hello to her together (p. 165). It doesn't stay nice long. Soon they start making mean remarks, saying that her hair smells like cod-liver oil (p. 165). "Being nice" was just a game to them, a way to show off their own importance and superiority. The saddest thing is that even a nice girl like Helen gets caught up in the game of superiority.
>
> In "Day of the Butterfly," Helen's main reason for being nice to Myra when they walk to school is to feel superior.

Here is the outline for the whole paper:

Thesis: Helen is nice to Myra on the way to school because it makes her feel superior.

Point 1: Myra makes Helen feel important.
   "magnanimous"
   Doesn't really feel friendly
   Lies about her brother
   Doesn't want her to wear the butterfly pin

Point 2: Helen does like Myra a little.
   Tells Myra she wants to be an airplane hostess
   Stands up to Miss Darling about Myra's birthday
   Thinks "why not" play with Myra

Point 3: The other girls also are nice to Myra to feel superior.
   Girls play "let's be nice to Myra" to show off
   The birthday party too—fancy wrappings
   Feel superior to Miss Darling as well as Myra
      "imitate" Miss D (p. 165)

Point 4: Myra is not deceived by the party.
   Feels "unexpected pride" (pp. 171-172)
   Acts superior to Gladys—"presided over" the party (p. 172)

Conclusion: Does Helen turn out to be worse to Myra because she deceives her?

Helen is the one she shares with and invites to play with her.

Nailing It Down

STRATEGY: CLUSTERING QUESTIONS AND IDEAS, PART 2

Your basic idea from the cluster you created will become your essay thesis. The other cluster ideas will form the theses of your supporting paragraphs. If you have lots of cluster ideas, you can divide them into groups and make each group a section of your essay.

You'll need to let your readers know what each paragraph or section is about as you begin it. Start by labeling how the cluster ideas relate to your basic idea. Then, when you write your paragraphs, use transitional words and phrases like the ones listed below to show these relationships to your readers.

HOW THE IDEA RELATES TO THE THESIS	TRANSITIONAL WORDS AND PHRASES
An example of the thesis	For example, . . . For instance, . . .
Part of a list of ideas that support the theses	Most important, . . . In addition, . . . Moreover, . . . First, ... Second, ... Third, ... Finally, . . .
An alternative to the thesis or a competing view	One possibility is . . . Another view is . . . On the one hand, ... On the other hand, . . .
A final conclusion about the thesis	On the whole, . . . Therefore, . . . In conclusion, . . .

Nailing It Down

DEMO: **CLUSTERING QUESTIONS AND IDEAS, PART 2**

After thinking about the questions in cluster 2 (page 74), the writer put together the following outline based on most of the cluster. The transitional phrases are included in brackets. Can you suggest some ways of incorporating the last few sentences from the cluster into the outline?

Introduction: Scrooge is really happy when he wakes up and finds out it's Christmas. Why does it matter so much if he plans to reform anyway?

Thesis: Christmas makes it possible for Scrooge to reform because everyone is kind and generous then.

Section 1 thesis: The Ghost of Christmas Present shows Scrooge the kindness and generosity of Christmas at his nephew's and at the Cratchits' houses.

> *Why is Scrooge so eager to join in the fun at his nephew's? It's catching. Just doing simple games and enjoying each other.*

> *[An even stronger example of Christmas kindness is . . .] the Cratchits are very poor but they are happy. Kind to each other and don't complain or get discouraged.*

Section 2 thesis: [In addition,] the Ghost of Christmas Present shows Scrooge how other people look down on his mean way of life without being harsh to him.

> *[For example, . . .] his nephew's comments show Scrooge that his meanness is foolish.*

> *[A more serious negative feeling is that . . .] Scrooge hears how the Cratchits dislike him in spite of their happiness.*

> *[On the other hand, . . .] there's hope because his nephew is sorry for Scrooge, not angry.*

> *The Cratchits [also] could become friendly because they do give the toast.*

Section 3 thesis: [Even] seeing the kindness of Christmas Past helps Scrooge reform.

Seeing Old Fezziwig makes Scrooge start wanting to be kind to Bob Cratchit, before he knows about Tiny Tim.

Add: [Also,] seeing the school boys reminds him to be kind to the carol singer, even though he himself was left alone at school for Christmas.

Section 4 thesis: [It is especially important that] Scrooge sees the kindness and generosity of Christmas because he had only a few happy times in his early life.

The Ghost of Christmas Past shows him how lonely his childhood was, left alone at school.

[Also,] the Ghost of Christmas Past shows him what he missed by not marrying.

Conclusion: [On the whole,] it seems really easy for Scrooge to reform. As soon as he wakes up, he begins, and he knows exactly what to do. This bothered me when I read the story, and it still bothers me because . . .

Writing: A Position Essay

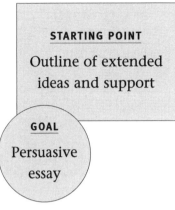

STARTING POINT

Outline of extended ideas and support

GOAL

Persuasive essay

ASSIGNMENT

Using your outline as a guide, present and argue for your position on an issue in a persuasive essay.

AUDIENCE

Students who have read the story, but do not necessarily share your ideas about it.

PURPOSE

To interest your readers in your way of understanding the story and to convince them to share it.

FORMAT

In three to six typed, double-spaced pages

* Introduce and explain the issue and why it interests you (one paragraph).

* State your position—your essay thesis—and clarify it (one paragraph).

* Explain and support with evidence all the aspects of your position one by one (three to six paragraphs).

* Examine alternative ideas and explain why you do not agree with them (one, two, or three paragraphs).

* Conclude by explaining a larger idea that follows from your position or by raising an unresolved question that your position suggests (one or two paragraphs).

SHOW YOUR WORK

Along with your essay, turn in

* Your journal

* Your first draft

* Your reader's questions and your notes from Testing It

CONVENTIONS TO MASTER

* Quoting or paraphrasing fairly ideas heard in discussion

* Using transitions to guide readers through complex ideas

* Drawing a conclusion for each section relating its paragraph theses to your essay thesis

For more guidance see the grading rubric on the next page (p. 86) and the sample student papers for A Position Essay (pp. 117–130).

Writing: A Position Essay

CONTENT/IDEAS

EXPERT (5) The essay illuminates the meaning of the story for the reader in a convincing way.

* The thesis is clear and distinctive and opens a new understanding of the story.

* Strong evidence from throughout the story is cited and is well explained.

* Alternative ideas are explained fully and fairly.

PRACTITIONER (3) The essay gives the reader some insight into the story that the reader is ready to agree with.

* The thesis is clear, though maybe rather simple, and suggests a way of understanding the story.

* Evidence is cited from a few parts of the story and some explanation is given.

* Alternative ideas are summarized.

BEGINNER (1) The essay does not add to the reader's understanding of the story.

* The thesis is unclear, obvious, or far-fetched.

* Evidence given is sparse and vague and not connected with the thesis.

* Alternative ideas are not recognized, and the position seems isolated.

ORGANIZATION

EXPERT (5) The essay explores an idea in an orderly way, with each part of the essay making its own contribution to the exploration.

* Paragraph theses are distinct, each contributing clearly to the essay thesis.

* Each paragraph presents and explains evidence that strongly supports its thesis.

* The introduction opens up the topic and essay thesis to the reader; the conclusion adds a final thought.

PRACTITIONER (3) The essay remains focused on an idea throughout, though there are some gaps and repetition in the exploration of it.

* Paragraph theses mostly differ from each other and are related to the thesis.

* Each paragraph cites evidence and relates it loosely to the thesis.

* The introduction states the topic and thesis and explains them in part; the conclusion may repeat an idea or abruptly close.

BEGINNER (1) The essay wanders or seems to lose track of the thesis; paragraphs leave ideas incomplete or repeat ideas.

* Paragraph theses are lacking, overly simple, or repeat or overlap each other.

* Some paragraphs lack support for their theses.

* The introduction simply states the topic and thesis and may restate them; the conclusion is lacking.

VOICE

EXPERT (5) The essay strongly engages the reader with the sense of an individual author committed to his or her ideas.

* The writer seems to explore his or her own thinking with sincerity and conviction.

* The writer seems to invite debate rather than closing it off.

PRACTITIONER (3) The essay gives the sense of a pleasant, well-intentioned writer.

* The writer seems to be partly engaged with his or her thinking and partly playing it safe.

* The writer shies away from confronting diverse ideas.

BEGINNER (1) The essay gives little sense of an individual writer standing behind it.

* The writer seems to be indifferent or going through the motions.

* The writer seems close-minded or unaware of other points of view.

WORD CHOICE

Apply your usual standards for word choice.

SENTENCE FLUENCY

Apply your usual standards for sentence fluency.

CONVENTIONS

Apply your usual standards for conventions.

PROCESS FOR THINKING AND WRITING

EXPERT (5) All steps of the process are chosen; questions and answers grow substantially at each stage in the process.

PRACTITIONER (3) Most steps of the process are shown; choices are made among questions and answers, and a few are added in later stages.

BEGINNER (1) Not enough of the process is shown to see how thinking progressed; questions and answers remain the same throughout.

7 Testing It

STARTING POINT

Draft of persuasive essay

GOAL

Constructive comments for revision

How do you know when you've made a good argument for your position? When people who have also thought about the issues think so! As soon as you have your full position in writing, team up with a partner to test each other's ideas.

WHEN YOU ARE THE READER, TESTING A DRAFT

* Try to understand your partner's position and accept it on its own terms.

* Read with curiosity, "talking back" to your partner's position, thinking of alternative ideas and looking for holes.

* Focus on important parts of your partner's position. No nitpicking!

* Write questions to clarify, to explain evidence, and to agree or disagree. Make your questions specific.

* Only ask questions—don't tell your partner what to think. Your partner's responses may surprise you!

WHEN YOU ARE THE WRITER, RESPONDING TO TESTING

* Make sure you understand your partner's question. Ask for clarification or support if needed.

* Take the question seriously and think it over.

* Respond in speech or writing. Explain or make changes in your position. (If you talk through your response, take notes.)

* Build the new ideas from your response into your next draft. Don't

  · Water down your ideas into harmless platitudes

  · Ignore questions

  · Tweak small details

  · Throw in support without explaining clearly its link with your position

Testing It

STRATEGY: **SHARPENING THE THESIS**

You've worked and worked on your essay thesis and the thesis statements for your supporting paragraphs, but still your partner might have questions. Since these statements are the foundation of your essay, it's worthwhile to address these problems:

* Thesis statement is a platitude, wishy-washy, something everyone would agree with. Your partner may ask: How does what you see in the story differ from what usually happens? What's special or unusual about it?

* Thesis statement uses a word or phrase that is confusing or vague and is not explained in the next few sentences. Your partner may ask: What do you mean by _____?

* Supporting paragraphs seem to be covering the same idea. Your partner may ask: How does the point of this paragraph thesis differ from that one? How are these two different aspects of the story?

IN YOUR NEXT DRAFT, RESPOND TO YOUR PARTNER'S QUESTIONS BY

* Explaining the thesis by going back to the question. Show where it came from, and why it interests you.

* Rethinking and re-explaining important statements.

* Checking paragraphs. Does each have a statement relating that paragraph to the thesis of the whole paper?

Testing It

DEMO: **SHARPENING THE THESIS**

Below are test questions for two of the paragraph theses from the outline of "The Diary of a Young Girl" on page 77. Try clarifying and explaining the theses in response to the questions.

> **PARAGRAPH THESIS:** Peter hides his true feelings from Anne because he is insecure.
>
> What do you mean by "insecure"?
>
> Why is Peter insecure in spite of his friendship with Anne?
>
> Where do you see that Anne can't sympathize with Peter's fears? Why can't she? Is she aware of this?
>
> **PARAGRAPH THESIS:** Another reason Peter feels insecure is that he is very upset about living in hiding.
>
> Anyone would be upset about hiding. In what way exactly is Peter upset?
>
> How do Peter's feelings about living in hiding differ from Anne's?

Testing It

STRATEGY 1: **STRENGTHENING SUPPORT**

Often support for a position needs to be beefed up; either there's not enough support or it's not well explained. Common problems include

1. Source passages seem ignored. Your partner may ask: Could this passage relate to your point? Was there a particular passage that made you think of your question?

2. Support is not explained or doesn't seem to add up to the thesis. Your partner may ask: How does this detail from the story support your thesis here? I'm not sure I got this connection—could you explain it more?

3. A strongly stated thesis still seems unconvincing. Your partner may ask: Are there other parts of the story where you see this? Does _____ (part of the story) show this, too?

IN YOUR NEXT DRAFT, RESPOND BY

* Explaining your support. Show how it leads to the thesis.

* Looking more closely at source passages to see how they relate to your position.

* Revisiting the whole story. Now that your essay thesis and paragraph theses are clear, story details will appear in a new light.

STRATEGY 2: **PULLING IT ALL TOGETHER**

When your group has gained some skill at testing, both asking questions and responding to them, arrange for several readers to respond to your essay.

Readers should try to present different points of view about the essay. Make a check mark to note when you agree with another reader's comment and then go on to a new point. Avoid focusing on just one paragraph or one kind of question.

Writers—don't be overwhelmed if your readers ask you lots of questions. Look for the common threads among them and address those in your next draft.

Testing It

DEMO: **PULLING IT ALL TOGETHER**

Below are four readers' questions about a passage from an essay on "Day of the Butterfly" and the writer's responses. Try responding as if you were the writer and the essay thesis were your own position.

THESIS

Helen at the end of the story realizes that it is unkind to act nice to someone just to make yourself feel superior.

PARAGRAPH OF SUPPORT

Myra thinks that <u>all the girls really like her,</u> that she is an "important" girl herself now. She smiles over the presents like she did over the butterfly pin because being important makes her happy. She isn't shy of the girls anymore, and she "presides" over the party. She feels so confident she <u>offers Helen the present.</u> It's a <u>way for her to be the superior one</u> for once. Myra invites Helen to play with her so they can always have that relationship. But <u>Helen feels she doesn't want the present if it means always being the inferior one.</u>

READER 1: If Myra thinks all the girls like her, why does she offer Helen the present? She has her choice of friends now. [Is the evidence explained?]

WRITER: Myra really likes Helen best. She isn't impressed by Gladys and the other important girls. Getting confident hasn't made her less sincere than she was.

or

Myra thinks Helen is a less important girl and so she'll be more likely to be her permanent friend.

READER 2: Does Myra want to be superior? Maybe she is just going along with the girls giving the party so they could be superior. She goes along with everything. She doesn't complain about having to be on the porch for recess. [Is the thesis on target?]

WRITER: Inviting Helen to play is the first time Myra does something for herself instead of just going along with what everyone else wants. Helen isn't sure she can still be superior to Myra now.

or

_____

_____

READER 3:   Did Helen only want to be superior? Didn't she do some things that seemed really friendly? She insisted Myra's birthday was in July in front of the whole class. [Is a source passage left out?]

WRITER: Helen likes Myra enough to be nice to her, but not enough to be her only friend. If you're the friend of an unpopular person, you end up being unpopular yourself.

or

_____

_____

READER 4:   Why does it say that Myra "and most of all her future" turned "shadowy" and "dark"? How does that fit in with what you are saying? [Is a source passage left out?]

WRITER: Myra's future is shadowy and dark because she might die. At the party, everyone was pretending that Myra was really okay. But the pretending has made Myra deceive herself about her future.

or

Myra's future is shadowy and dark because she knows she might die. She knows that's why they had her "birthday" in March. She wants to reassure Helen because she knows it would be hard to be friends with someone who is dying.

or

_____

_____

8 Putting It Out There

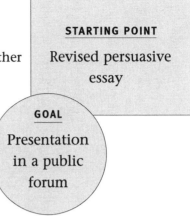

STARTING POINT

Revised persuasive essay

GOAL

Presentation in a public forum

Most writers love to be read. Most readers love to share with another reader a story they loved—or hated. How do you set up these opportunities?

Your classmates and teacher are a natural audience not only because they are convenient (in fact, inescapable!) but also because they have shared the process of reading, discussing, and writing with you.

Perhaps the most important audience for your thinking is—you. Let the ideas you've developed from reading flavor your life and make you aware of greater meaning in everyday events. And, enjoy the feeling of having grown an idea from seed to full flowering.

Putting It Out There

STRATEGIES

Because *A Christmas Carol* is a famous, well-loved story, there is a big audience for your ideas about this story. They'll want to respond to your ideas and tell you theirs, too!

* Hold a symposium on *A Christmas Carol* for other students, parents, teachers, and community members. Ask participants to read the story or watch one of the movies made from the story. Set up workshops on different issues in the story in which participants can read or state their positions and exchange views.

* Create a Web site on *A Christmas Carol*. Post your positions and include an e-mail address for visitors to respond.

* Watch one of the movies based on *A Christmas Carol*. Discuss how well it expresses the issues in the story that you consider most interesting.

* Watch two or three other Christmas movies. Discuss how the ideas about Christmas you see in them agree with or differ from those of *A Christmas Carol*.

* If ideas from *A Christmas Carol* have made an impression on you, consider ways you might act on them. Try adding to your Christmas or other holiday customs or to your everyday habits at home or at school.

Sample Student Papers

Sample Student Papers

Grading

Each set of student papers corresponds to a writing assignment from *The Reader Writes*. The grading of these papers is based on the rubric for each assignment, focusing on Content, Organization, and Voice. The papers are followed by comments a teacher might write to help the student better understand his or her essay's strengths and weaknesses.

Not every paper with strong content, organization, and voice is equally strong in word choice, sentence fluency, and conventions. Most teachers will want to score for these traits, too. Still, the ideas in an essay are what make it worth reading.

USING QUESTIONS TO REVISE STUDENT WRITING

What questions do you have about the essay? That is, honest questions—those to which you really want to hear the writer's answers, instead of rhetorical or leading questions. Usually the most interesting parts of the essay raise questions, although these parts may also be unclear or confusing.

Questions about interesting but puzzling parts of an essay show a writer where an argument can be strengthened. Instead of simply "correcting," invite the writer to develop his or her paper further.

Use Reading for Questions strategies when reading and responding to papers.

Writing: An Open Question

Sample 1

Why was he mad at Nicky Carver for stealing his secret? On page 19 it says, "It took a long time but he did in the end. I smiled at him. He had stolen my secret. He looked away."

I think that the narrator was mad at Nicky for fessing up. The narrator wanted to always be the one that took the books. Now that Nicky confessed it's not the narrator's secret anymore. They all think Nicky Carver did it.

GRADE

CONTENT—1

The question as it is stated seems to have only one possible answer, since anyone is mad when someone "steals" something from him.

ORGANIZATION—1

The writer has only one answer, but does explain it.

VOICE—3

The writer sounds businesslike and direct, though rather brusque.

QUESTIONS TO REVISE STUDENT WRITING

What's behind your question? Were you surprised that he was mad at Nicky? Were you unsure what he meant by "he had stolen my secret"?

Why does the narrator feel that he's lost his secret, even though no one but Nicky will ever know that he stole the books?

Sample 2

Dom Francis was speaking. " 'As you can see,' he said, 'the exercise books have not been returned.' " When I saw that on page 13, I knew the narrator didn't return the exercise books. Why didn't he?

I don't think the narrator wanted to return the books because he wanted to prove to himself that he could do something bad and get away with it. He could have wanted to keep the books as a souvenir. The narrator probably didn't want to turn them in because all his classmates were mean to him and never wanted to play with him so he decided to punish them for that. Maybe the narrator was really mean at heart but seemed nice to everyone else.

GRADE

CONTENT—2

This is a genuine question with several interesting answers.

ORGANIZATION—2

The writer does a little to explain where the question comes from. She suggests four different, interesting answers, but simply lists them. None of the answers is explained.

VOICE—4

The writer sounds direct and decisive, though a little hasty. She is "on" for the entire piece of writing, though it is short.

QUESTIONS TO REVISE STUDENT WRITING

Since the narrator is the thief, he would have told about returning the books, if he had decided to do so. Why did you focus on the passage in which Dom Francis says that he'll have to punish the class?

There could be at least one question about each of the answers, since none is explained: For example, why is the narrator "getting away" with doing something bad, if he gets punished for it along with the rest of the class? What would the books have been a "souvenir" of?

Sample 3

In school we have been reading a book called "I Just Kept on Smiling." From this book I only have one question and that is why did Nicky Carver say that he took the exercise books? If he were going to do something I don't get why he did it so late instead of earlier. If I were him I would have either done nothing at all or told on the main character, instead of saying it was I. In the next three paragraphs I will explain my question with three different answers.

One reason may be that Nicky wanted to make Dom Francis feel better. But he also didn't want the main character to tell on himself. The reason why he didn't want the main character to tell on himself was because he would have been forced to. He even told him not to. Since Nicky knew that and also wanted to make Dom Francis feel better, he could only do one thing—tell on himself. That would be my first answer to my question.

A second reason may be that Nicky wanted to be the bad guy for once, instead of always being the good boy. He knew the main character wasn't going to turn himself in, so he thought he could be bad. He said he stole the books and at the same time stole the main character's secret and would never give it back. This is another explanation.

A third reason may be that Nicky wanted to show an example of being good to the main character. This way if he ever did it again for some strange reason and didn't get told to turn himself in maybe he would do it by himself. He also took the main character's secret to teach him a lesson along with showing an example of what to do. This is the last explanation that I have for my one question.

In conclusion my question was why did Nicky Carver say that he took the exercise books. I have found three answers for it using my mind and the book. The three answers, were Nicky wanted to make Dom Francis feel better but he also didn't want the main character to tell on himself, or that Nicky wanted to be the bad guy for once, instead of always being the good boy, or even that Nicky wanted to show an example of being good to the main character. Those were my answers. If you were to read this story you might get the same or different answers, but it is up to you.

CONTENT—4

The writer explains the topic question enough to make the reader see that it really is a puzzle. The three possible answers gave the reader distinct perspectives on the problem.

ORGANIZATION—3

The paragraphs each explain an answer; the first and second answers were unclear in places. The conclusion simply repeats ideas already more clearly stated before.

VOICE—3

Once the writer gets started (after the second sentence), she sounds confident and engaged within each paragraph. But each paragraph ends with a dull, conventional statement that distracts the reader from the ideas themselves. The final paragraph also pushes the reader away. When first "meeting" the reader and when "signing off," inexperienced writers often lose their poise!

QUESTIONS TO REVISE STUDENT WRITING

Why would Dom Francis feel better to have someone confess to taking the exercise books, when he has already punished everyone?

When you say that Nicky admitted to stealing the books and stole the main character's secret, do you mean that confessing and stealing the secret were the same? If so, why are they the same? Is Nicky trying to be a bad guy toward the main character or the rest of the school?

Sample 4

"I Just Kept On Smiling" by Simon Burt is about a guy who's in private school, and lives there. He throws away his birthday cards, and goes to chapel, which people think is weird. He has a friend named Nicky Carver. The main character stole books, and then he tore them up. Everything in the story is fine, but there is one big fact that just doesn't belong there: Nicky Carver said that he stole the books. Nicky knew that wasn't him, he knew that his friend did it. Why did Nicky Carver take the responsibility for the books?

I read this story several times and each time I came up with a different answer. First, I thought that this fact has something to do with Nicky's religion. His brother is studying to be a priest. Maybe his faith didn't let him live with feeling that he knows who stole the books. He couldn't think about anything else beside that. He was probably shocked that his best friend actually stole something. He couldn't live with it, and he told the teacher to get punished to keep from having to live with the guilt. Also, taking responsibility will stop the others from beating up his friend.

Then I heard a totally different answer in class. Maybe Nicky just wanted to see what it feels like to be a bad kid. Well, Nicky never steals. He is not tough like some of the others. He's an ordinary kid just like the narrator. If the narrator took the books because he was tired of being a boring, good kid, Nicky might have felt the same way. Maybe he wanted to see what it feels like to get a reputation as a bad kid without even doing the crime.

When I thought about Nicky Carver in another way, I realized that Nicky might have done it to help his friend. How? Well, by showing the consequences of stealing. Nicky wanted to show the main character that stealing is not a good thing, and by taking the responsibility Nicky showed the main character what will happen if he steals again. He knows he won't get away with it, because Nicky has as good as told him he knows he is the thief.

This question has a lot of different answers. I've told you my three, but there may be more! Maybe you'll find another answer to this question. What do you think? Why did Nicky Carver take the responsibility of stealing the exercise books?

CONTENT—5

The question is certainly central to the story. This essay gives more than three answers if you count the suggestion that Nicky confessed to keep the others from beating up the narrator. They are all quite different, make sense, and give different perspectives on the story.

ORGANIZATION—4

Each of the answers is clearly explained in its own paragraph. The idea behind each is laid out so they all seem quite reasonable. The question itself is not so fully explained; the summary of the story at the beginning does not seem to lead up to the question.

VOICE—4

This writer sounds alert and interested, like someone thinking out loud with the reader. It isn't necessary to refer to rereading the story and to hearing another answer in class. The writer comes across as a real, thinking person with words like "maybe," "probably," and by laying out the whole train of thought for the reader.

QUESTIONS TO REVISE STUDENT WRITING

When you summarize the narrator's "weird" behavior and how he steals the books and then tears them up, why do you say, "everything in the story is fine"? Why does Nicky's "weird" behavior in confessing seem to you more of a question than the narrator's weird behavior? (Answering this might help you explain your question more.)

If Nicky is trying to deal with his shock and guilt that his friend was the thief, why would he be interested in protecting his friend from being beaten up by the other boys?

If Nicky takes responsibility in order to help his friend, do you think it is to show his friend the consequences of stealing or to threaten that he might tell on his friend the next time?

$\mathcal{W}riting$: Exploring an Issue

Sample 1

Why was Louie so concerned about managing Howie's baseball team to be the best they could be?

Remember the nerd back in grade school that would do anything and everything to receive the attention of his or her peers? The geek is always so quiet and so smart, so why would he or she risk their own schoolwork just to be popular?

"For the next few weeks Louie was the busiest guy in the world—calling up guys from other schools, arranging games, getting permits from the park department, talking to George and keeping him happy, coming to our practices. . . . when he started giving us suggestions on things, nobody objected either. He may have been a lousy ball player, but I'll say this for him, he knew more about the game than any of us." (p. 49)

Louie didn't care what extreme measures he had to go through, he wanted to be popular! No matter which way you slice it, it still remains, Louie wants to be noticed as the Zodiacs' manager.

Louie couldn't play baseball well, even though he knew more about it than anyone on the team. You would think to be a manager, you would at least know how to play the sport.

Plain and simple Louie was a loner. It did not matter how smart he was until he put his brain to good use. Coming up with the idea of being manager, and playing the Star Spangled Banner at the games was a good idea to get his team noticed. That is exactly what he had in mind. Once he got the Zodiacs noticed it would no longer be Howie's team, it would be Louie's. The idea he came up with about using George as a pitcher, and bait for the press, that surprised everyone.

Louie's plan worked and resulted in him being popular.

GRADE

CONTENT—1

The writer only offers one thesis—that Louie did this to become popular, which seems to be contradicted by the statements that Louie is a "loner," and that he doesn't know enough about the sport to be a manager. The thesis is also contradicted by the question, "why would he or she risk their own schoolwork just to become popular?"

ORGANIZATION—1

The paper rambles because the topic question is not well developed enough for the writer to keep track of it.

VOICE—2

The voice is inconsistent—sometimes direct and engaging, sometimes argumentative and sarcastic.

QUESTIONS TO REVISE STUDENT WRITING

Why would Louie risk his schoolwork and his other hobbies in order to manage the team? Why is popularity so important to him?

Why does Louie recruit George to make the team outstanding, instead of just concentrating on making the games more fun for boys like Howie and Izzy, so he could be popular with them?

Does Louie become popular as a result of managing the team?

Sample 2

After reading "The Zodiacs" by Jay Neugeboren, I wondered why Louie went after George at the end of the story. That is when Louie told George he only owed $8. I believe Louie went after George because he thought it was best for the team, himself, and George.

It was good for the team for Louie to go after George because they knew they couldn't win without him. "That was the last time we had the lead, though. The Raiders tied it up in the third inning, and went ahead in the fourth, by 4-1. The final score was 7-2." This game was played without George and they lost.

George and his gang tell Louie and the team, "'We'll get you guys at school.'" This shows it is best for Louie to go after George for himself so he doesn't get beat up.

It was best for Louie to go after George, for George too. Louie knew he was better than just another gang member, and he knew he had potential to be very good at sports, but he just didn't like being told what to do. "The coaches and teachers were always talking to him about going straight and being a star in high school and college. But George never seemed to care much." George doesn't listen to his teachers when they tell him he is a good athlete. He needs someone else to tell him in a different way, which Louie does!

Even though at the end of the story George and his brother Vinnie run off to Florida, for a short time Louie helps himself, the team, and George.

Sharing Questions Chart

Question

Why did Louie go after George at the end of the story?

Answer 1	Answer 2	Answer 3
He knew the Zodiacs needed George to win	He didn't want to get beat up by George	Making George feel like he won by apologizing because George is stubborn—doesn't like to be told what to do Knows George is more than a gang member—has potential
TEAM "The final score was 7-2." Can't win without George	HIMSELF "We—we don't need crooks on the Zodiacs. Get out." " 'I—I didn't mean to call you that,' said Louie. 'Why don't we just forget the whole thing?' " "We'll get you guys at school."	GEORGE "The coaches and teachers were always talking to him about going straight . . ."

CONTENT—2

The topic question is unclear; we aren't told why it would be surprising or puzzling that Louie went after George. The essay assumes that this was the thing to do, although in the story it looks as if Louie struggles to do it. The evidence too is not clearly related to the theses being proved. The quotations from the story show the problems Louie faced, but they don't show why Louie would have acted the way he did to solve them.

ORGANIZATION—3

Clear but very simple organization. The introduction simply states the topic question; then each paragraph takes on a different idea and supports it in a simple way.

VOICE—3

The voice doesn't have too much personality, but it also is not self-conscious or indifferent.

QUESTIONS TO REVISE STUDENT WRITING

Most of the questions are about making connections between the points in the paper and the notes. It's not uncommon for a beginning writer to have good ideas in notes that never get included in the paper. Most of the following questions are about connecting the notes to points in the essay, so that the essay can include more of what the writer actually thinks.

In your notes, you include passages where Louie tells George to get out and then apologizes to George. Why didn't you include these in your paper? Do you think that Louie changed his mind in dealing with George? If so, why?

In your notes, you mention George's stubbornness—he doesn't like to be told what to do. Do you think that Louie was aware of this? Was it something that shaped Louie's decision to go after George?

Why are you surprised or interested that Louie went after George?

Did your ideas about why Louie went after George change your understanding of the story? (Answering this could help you write a more interesting conclusion.)

Sample 3

" 'Okay,' said George. 'But he better hurry. I got better things to do than spend all day strikin' out a bunch of fags.' " If George felt so badly about playing on the Zodiacs, then why did he join in the first place? My answers to this question are that he knows that it can be his start to fame. Another is that he wants to prove that he is better than the other kids. And last, he likes to play baseball, but he thinks he has to hide it because he is trying to be cool and tough like his older brother, Vinnie. I will explain these answers more in this essay.

" 'Simple,' said Louie. 'I offered him the one thing that he couldn't refuse—fame.' " This is a perfect example on why George could have joined the baseball team. Louie knew that George wanted fame, and he used that to convince George to join the team to be their pitcher. Louie told George that he could get his name in the newspaper, and George knew that was a good way to get famous. And you can tell that George wants fame, too. In the book it says, "Whenever he wanted an audience, George would sit down on the steps of the school—on Rogers Avenue—and start telling tales of the jobs he and Vinnie had pulled off." So if George was so determined to be famous, then he joined the Zodiacs to make his dream a reality. He wanted to get in the newspaper for doing something he was really good at—baseball.

I also think that George wants to show that he is better than all of the other kids. At the beginning when I mentioned how he said that he had better things to do that fits into this answer, too. He calls the other kids names, he doesn't go to practices, and he is obviously making a statement. He definitely doesn't think that the kids are worth practicing with. But he has a strange way of showing it. Instead of refusing the offer of being the pitcher of the Zodiacs, he does join, but just to show everybody there up. He doesn't want anybody messing with him. He shows his teammates that he is better than them by pitching winning games. He clearly thinks that he is better than everyone else.

And last, but not least, he actually likes to play baseball, but he wants to be like his big brother, Vinnie. Like in my reason on how he wants to be famous, whenever he wanted an audience, he tells of the things he and his brother had pulled off. Obviously he respects his brother and wants to be like him. If he didn't, then he wouldn't brag about him so much and include himself in his stories of his brother. So George tries to be like Vinnie. He really likes to play baseball, but he wants to be like his brother and doesn't want to admit it. In George's eyes, his brother, Vinnie, is the greatest.

So in conclusion, my answers to this question were that he wants to become famous, he wants to prove that he is better than everyone else, and last, he likes baseball but just doesn't want to admit it because he is trying to be like his brother. I think that my best reason was my first one: George wants to be famous.

That one has the most evidence from the book and I think is the clearest to see. He is determined to become famous so he does it through a baseball team, the Zodiacs. I think there are many possible answers to this question, and I know that mine were well thought out and good. I also know that mine were only a few of the possible answers. I'm sure that you can find out some for yourself.

GRADE

CONTENT—3

The point that George thinks he is better than the others is very well supported with a lot of separate facts from the story. There is less evidence for the point that George is seeking fame—just Louie's belief that that is what motivated George. There is no support for the idea that George really likes to play baseball, although the point that he wants to be like Vinnie is supported.

ORGANIZATION—4

Each paragraph covers a distinct point, and all strongly address the topic question. Because two paragraphs rely on evidence that the writer introduces earlier to support other ideas, the evidence is not equally strong for all of the paragraphs.

VOICE—3

This paper starts out very confidently with an interesting quotation, and the three answers are discussed in a lively way. But the final paragraph sounds very self-conscious and detached.

QUESTIONS TO REVISE STUDENT WRITING

Louie says that he offered George fame if he would play with the Zodiacs, but how are you sure that this was George's major reason for joining the team?

If George wants to show the rest of the team that he is better than they are, why does he join them in selling raffle tickets?

Sample 4

"The Zodiacs" is about a young team, and their manager Louie has big dreams. He wants to make his team famous. He tries, and they get a little fame, such as scores posted in the newspaper, one article in the newspaper, and many people coming to watch their games. The team was good, and never lost a game. But the reason they keep winning is their pitcher, a big bully named George. Louie, the manager, tells him he owes $12 for a raffle the team is doing. Louie tells him he can't play in their next game if he doesn't pay the money. George doesn't pay, so they lose their next game badly. Louie tells George that he made a mistake and says he only owes $8, not $12. But since Louie is so smart, I doubt this is true. I think Louie admits to making a mistake he didn't make in order to save the team.

Even though I believe Louie didn't make a mistake, it's possible he could have. He said, "I discovered I made a mistake yesterday. You really owed eight dollars." He said he made a mistake, so it's possible that he did. Louie can figure out baseball batting averages in his head, so why would he make a simple mistake like that? But Louie is also very honest. He told Howie he knew he was not a good baseball player. So he might be honest about the money, too.

Or, Louie could have told George he only owed $8 because he was scared. Before Louie told George, all of the boys got into a fight with George and his gang. Then the cops showed up, and as George and his gang were leaving he said, "We'll get you guys at school," but then the cops stopped him. So I think Louie may have been scared, and told George that so George wouldn't be so mad. Just before the fight, when George and his gang were coming toward him, Louie told George that he hadn't meant to call him a liar and a crook, even though at the time Louie did mean it. This was also because Louie was scared, for himself and for his team.

What I most believe was behind Louie's actions was that Louie knew his team needed George to win. And if he told George that he had been wrong, then George would be happy to come back and play. Also, by lowering the price he could get George to pay and come back instead of Louie having to beg him to come back without him paying at all. The game George didn't play went like this: "The Raiders tied it up in the third inning, and went ahead in the fourth, by 4-1. The final score was 7-2." They were so used to winning, and once George was gone they lost. So they learned how much they needed George.

Even though Louie could have made a mistake, I don't think he did because Louie's so smart. He could have been afraid of George, but I don't think that's the case because I think Louie's very brave, like when he talks to George after the fight. But I do think Louie wanted to play a big role on his team by helping them win, and getting George back on the team is one way of doing that.

CONTENT—4

Even though the writer prefers one of the paragraph theses, all of them are well supported. The writer cites evidence that covers many aspects of the story, especially pertaining to Louie's character. Throughout the paper, the reader gets a clear sense that this is a question worth considering.

ORGANIZATION—4

Each paragraph explores a different point which is supported with evidence from the text. The paragraphs are also clearly related to each other as the writer seems to argue back and forth about each. But the point about Louie's courage, made in the conclusion, fits more logically with the paragraph that discusses how Louie might have been scared of George.

VOICE—4

The paper is written clumsily, but nonetheless the writer discusses ideas with the reader.

QUESTIONS TO REVISE STUDENT WRITING

Since Louie knew that a good pitcher was important to the team, why did he demand that George pay the twelve dollars or leave the team? In other words, why didn't Louie change it to eight dollars when the boys were settling up their raffle tickets?

How does talking to George after the fight show that Louie's brave? Didn't you argue that Louie might have talked with George to keep him from carrying out his threat of getting the boys at school? Do you think that Louie is brave at other times in the story?

Sample 5

Why is it significant for us as readers to know Louie's hobbies? Several reasons help to give you a better understanding of the story. The character introduction and background provides us with these hobbies which is important for our knowledge of Louie and the role he plays in the story. Also, Louie's hobbies are a back-up as to how and why Howie says that Louie is an "interesting guy." Louie's hobbies also give us a view into how motivated and determined he is to be involved in baseball although he isn't athletic. They show how Louie has what it takes to be a great general manager.

At the beginning of "The Zodiacs" Louie's hobbies are significant in bringing in the character. This is vital to the story because it creates a certain image of that character. For example, in the very beginning of the story Howie says, "I knew lots about Louie that nobody in school knew" (p. 44). This is important to the significance of the background because this statement creates a certain feeling inside of you.

When Howie says that Louie is an "interesting guy" it leads you to wonder what he means by this. But as the story unfolds and Louie's hobbies are revealed, you learn that Howie means this in a positive way and that he admires Louie. Also, Howie continually talks through pride, instead of just an ordinary voice that isn't "loud" enough. One example of this that is very clear is when he says, "What amazed me most about Louie, though, was that he could figure out a player's batting average in his head" (p. 45). Another example of his pride is toward the end when the team, including Howie, tries to fight George Santini, not only for themselves but to stand up for Louie also. These examples relate to Louie's being an "interesting guy" because from Howie's tone and actions you realize that he most definitely admires Louie.

Louie's hobbies include a lot of work. For instance, taking care of tropical fish. Howie also says, "I don't know how many days he'd waited outside of Ebbets Field to get them, all I know is he had the best collection of baseball players' signatures of any guy in school" (p. 45). This is very important because it compares him to the other guys in school.

When he becomes general manager, Louie does a lot of hard work. Howie says he is "calling up guys at other schools, arranging games, getting permits from the park department" (p. 49). These things are not fun like having practice games together with your team. Louie also sets up the raffle and gets the uniform company to trust him with the money for the uniforms. It shows you along with the others that Louie is a very determined person.

Another point about Louie's hobbies is that they are something different and imaginative. He collects Chinese puzzles, which most people have never heard of. Magic tricks you have to practice and also be kind of smart to make them really work. Probably lots of people collect baseball players' autographs, but Louie also does things that are more out of the way. He is the same way when he becomes general manager of the Zodiacs. He brings a cassette player to the games to play the "Star Spangled Banner." He calls a newspaper and tells them the team scores, and the newspaper prints them. These are things that a kid or even an adult wouldn't usually think up unless they had a lot of imagination.

When you learn Louie's hobbies at the beginning of the story you automatically stereotype Louie as a nerd, when he is just the opposite. He is an "interesting guy" as Howie calls him, and that is why he makes the Zodiacs into a great team. Howie and the rest of the team know this, and they follow his leadership and also fight to defend him. Even George appreciates being on the team in a way. Louie has the motivation just in himself to fill the night sky with shimmering stars.

GRADE

CONTENT—5

This essay's topic question grew from the question, "Why does Louie have such boring hobbies?" The writer has developed this question into something far from boring that changes the way a reader thinks about the story. The question is not very well explained in the introduction, but the subsequent paragraphs all help answer it with evidence from throughout the story. The conclusion adds a new idea about Louie's "leadership."

It's especially fun to read an essay using a really unusual question.

ORGANIZATION—4

The paragraph theses are clear and distinct, and each one is supported with evidence from the story—most from several parts of the story. Their order seems logical, although sometimes we seem to jump from idea to idea.

VOICE—3

The essay starts off sounding detached and artificial; later it sounds like the writer is working hard to present these ideas and is maybe somewhat unsure. These problems are a result of tackling a hard question.

QUESTIONS TO REVISE STUDENT WRITING

Why does the author want the readers to know that Louie was an "interesting guy" at the beginning of the story, instead of letting us discover it the way his teammates did?

Why does the author point out that Louie's teammates don't know how interesting he is when he first becomes their manager?

When the other players help Louie fight George, does this reflect their pride in Louie?

Does Louie's imagination, as expressed in his hobbies, affect his ability to deal with George?

What feeling is created inside of you when reading Howie's statement, "I knew lots about Louie that nobody in school knew"?

Writing: A Position Essay

Sample 1

A gift of friendship is cherished when you are lower in the social chain and aren't really given that friendship and love anywhere else. When Helen gave Myra the gift Helen insisted that she keep it because she wanted her to feel like she was special and wanted. Helen wanted her to feel that she was gaining a friend and moving up from the bottom.

When Helen gave the cheap Cracker Jack pin to Myra she wanted her to feel needed as a friend because she knew she was higher than Myra. "I had often loitered in that way, wanting to walk with some important girl who was behind me, and not quite daring to stop and wait."(pg 166) Helen wanted Myra to feel like she was a friend and the pin symbolized that friendship. Myra was below Helen but Helen didn't want her to feel that way.

I think Helen also feels that she needs to give love and attention to Myra because she might not get it anywhere else. "I couldn't afford to be seen walking with her, and I did not even want to—but, on the other hand, the flattery of those humble, hopeful turnings was not lost on me." Helen wanted Myra to be that girl that got stopped and talked to.

Also when Myra gets sick and they come to visit her, Myra gives Helen a present back to her. I think Myra did this because she really had never gotten a present before and she wanted to repay Helen for the pin. Myra said, "I got too many things. You take something."

So in conclusion Helen wanted Myra to know that she wasn't at the bottom and just stuck here on earth for no good reason.

CONTENT—1

This paper answers the question, "Why does Helen give Myra the butterfly pin and walk to school with her?" The answer that Helen wants to be kind seems true as far as it goes, but it doesn't seem to take into account the conflict that Helen feels about her interactions with Myra. The idea is scarcely developed; the paragraphs bring up just two different incidents in the story, without considering an alternative idea, and the conclusion simply repeats part of the introduction.

ORGANIZATION—1

Two paragraphs seem to make the same point about Helen stopping Myra on the way to school. The writer doesn't provide the necessary evidence showing that Helen's motive is kindness rather than something else.

VOICE—2

This paper starts out strongly but seems to lose steam. By the conclusion, it seems as if the writer had lost interest.

QUESTIONS TO REVISE STUDENT WRITING

How does the "cheap Cracker Jack pin" make Myra feel needed as a friend?

Why does Helen keep on feeling "higher" than Myra? Is Helen's wanting Myra to "feel like she was a friend" the same as Helen's really being Myra's friend?

Are there other times in the story when Helen shows that she wants to be kind to Myra? Are there times when she doesn't?

You say that Myra wants to "repay" Helen for the butterfly pin. Do you mean that she feels Helen is her friend or that she owes Helen a debt?

Sample 2

While reading "The Day of the Butterfly" by Alice Munro, many questions popped in my head, and this is the one that I have chosen to write my paper on. When the author says, "A role was shaping for me that I could not resist playing" (Munro pg. 166 para.2), what is the role that is shaping for Helen?

I believe the role that is shaping for Helen is the role of a more dominant character or a character higher up the food chain than Myra. I believe Helen is a bit starved of not knowing enough about the ever-growing enigma that is Myra Sayla, and Helen believes she can wedge herself in Myra's life, and really get to know her. I believe Helen's intentions are good, just to get to know Myra.

The first bit of evidence I have of my thesis is at the very beginning of the story, when the narrator, Helen, could explain the intricacies of Myra's little brother Jimmy's wetting problem. Perhaps Helen had a secret interest in getting to know Myra, something that goes beyond the text.

My next bit of proof is while walking to school, the way that Helen quickened her pace to walk with Myra even though she didn't want to be seen walking with her and risked being seen anyway. Again she is watching Myra carefully as she looks back on the road.

Some other people probably believe that Helen walks with Myra simply to make her happy. I strongly disagree with this because if that statement was so then why did Helen want to go to Myra's birthday party? That could have been unpleasant and upsetting for Myra. Why did Helen stay with Myra even after the bell had rung that visitor time was over, but not want to take the present? And to conclude why I disagree so strongly with that thesis, why did Helen walk to school even though she didn't really want to be seen with her? Making someone else happy is not a strong enough reason. The answer is because Helen was mesmerized by Myra's undesire to be cool, popular or anything like that. Myra does not have the worries and fears that follow Helen everywhere.

To end my paper I would like to throw a question out on the table. If all of the previously stated was correct, then did Myra ever have a desire to get to know Helen, or anyone for that matter? Did Helen have it all wrong when she thought that Myra was looking back at her like she was more important? She could have been flattering herself, making herself more important than she was. Perhaps Helen was the outcast the whole time, and Myra understood everyone's feelings towards her.

CONTENT—2

This starts with two ideas that seem contradictory: Helen wanted to be more important than Myra, and Helen simply wanted to find out what kind of person Myra was. The idea of Helen being curious about Myra is interesting, but the evidence for it needs more explanation. Ideas are sparking in this paper, and they deserve more development.

ORGANIZATION—2

Each paragraph is given a separate point to prove. However, most of the paragraphs just allude to a fact in the story; few explain what the facts mean and how they support the writer's ideas. Some paragraphs are unclear.

VOICE—4

After the first paragraph, the writer sounds engaged and even excited about the ideas. There are some eloquent phrases here that engage the reader.

QUESTIONS TO REVISE STUDENT WRITING

Does "getting to know Myra" help Helen be a "dominant character"? How?

How do you know that Myra is an "ever-growing enigma" to Helen?

Why isn't being kind a strong enough reason for Helen to walk with Myra?

Sample 3

The story "Day of the Butterfly" by Alice Munro had many hidden messages intertwined throughout the tale. The most interesting issue to me can be summed up in one question. Why will people go along with, or follow, a crowd? Even when they know that the crowd is doing something morally wrong, they still won't object or speak out. When the crowd is persecuting someone simply because that person is different from them, what would be the consequences of following your heart instead of the crowd? Would it be too risky to speak out and say, "Hey, this is wrong"?

I believe people go along with a crowd mainly out of fear. I think they may want to be kind to the person that the crowd is mocking, but they are too afraid. When a crowd is making fun of someone who is not like them, they are also ostracizing that person. If anyone were to speak out against the crowd's actions, they only subject themselves to being ostracized too. It's easier and safer to follow the crowd even if it is out of fear. After all, there's safety in numbers!

In this story Helen was conflicted with wanting to befriend Myra, who was the outsider, and not being different from the crowd. She was afraid to be seen walking to school with Myra. "I could not afford to be seen walking with her . . . " (Munro p. 166). Although she was flattered that Myra had slowed down and was glancing back in hopes that Helen would catch up to her, Helen couldn't help but think of what the crowd would say if they saw them walking together. " . . . the flattery of those humble, hopeful turnings was not lost on me." (Munro p. 166). In this instance, Helen broke away from the crowd somewhat because she did walk with Myra. However, Helen was in constant fear of the consequences of being seen with her.

As the story continued, Helen offered Myra another gesture of kindness, and again Helen was consumed with thoughts of the crowd discovering her kind gesture. She gave Myra the butterfly brooch from the Cracker Jack box, and "Myra put the brooch in her pocket." (Munro p. 168). Helen was relieved when she did that. "I was glad she had not put it on. If someone asked her where she got it, and she told them, what would I say?" (Munro p. 169). Helen was afraid to admit that she had been kind to someone who the crowd had dictated everyone should be rude to.

At the end of the story, Myra wanted to repay Helen for her kindness by giving her a leatherette case. Once again, Helen thought she shouldn't accept the case because she didn't want to be forced to explain to the crowd why Myra gave it to her. "I didn't want to take the case now but I could not think how to get out of it, what lie to tell." (Munro p. 173). Helen was afraid that the crowd might think they were friends. And where would that leave Helen?

More often than not, I think a crowd will be mean to someone just to try to look cool. It might make them feel like they are better than the person they are trying to degrade. And they probably think they're not really hurting that person. However, I believe that the crowd is leaving lifelong, emotional scars on their victims. In the story Myra and her brother were victims of the crowd. Their emotional scars could be seen in their outward appearances. "Whenever you happened to look at them their heads were slightly bent, their narrow bodies hunched in . . . Over their dark eyes the lids were never fully raised; they had a weary look." (Munro p. 163) So the power of the crowd that Helen feared so much was great.

After I finished reading the story and thought about everything that had happened, a sickening thought came to mind. I realized that the crowd was only nice to Myra after they had found out she was sick and going to die. By this time their gestures of kindness were too little and too late. They couldn't undo the emotional damage that they had caused. Then I started to think about all the times people are honored, or given an award, after they've passed away. By this time don't you think it's too little, too late?

GRADE

CONTENT—3

The essay begins with a question about why people follow the crowd and then shows why Helen does, out of fear. A question open to more possible answers would have given the paper a better foundation, so that it could consider exactly what this fear is and why Helen sometimes defied it. Some of the paragraphs prove the same point; each idea is supported with evidence. The most interesting point for this reader was the second to last paragraph, which strongly supports the idea that Myra and her brother suffer from the way they are treated.

ORGANIZATION—2

After the introduction and thesis statement (first two paragraphs), the paragraphs seem loosely connected. They seem to follow in order of the story—retelling it, rather than in order of ideas.

VOICE—3

The writing carries conviction, but it does not seem to invite readers to join the writer in thinking through the problem.

QUESTIONS TO REVISE STUDENT WRITING

Why does Helen sometimes offer Myra a gesture of kindness, even though Helen is actually committed to going along with the crowd?

How does the crowd (the rest of the girls) influence Helen? How do they get across to her their message?

Why does Helen say that she "didn't want the case now"? What has changed "now" for her with regard to Myra?

Why is it easy for the crowd to be nice to Myra when she's dying, but hard for Helen?

Sample 4

"The Day Of The Butterfly" by Alice Munro represents a situation that toys with the mind and makes it bend and shape to understand even a small piece of it. That situation is the type of friendship that exists between Helen and Myra. The question of whether Helen really wants to be Myra's friend or not is where the real emotion comes out in this story.

At the start, Myra seems to be a character that could quickly and easily grab the lead role with the story starting with "when Myra Sayla came to town" (Munro 162). With this statement, the reader expects that Myra is the main character. This seems true since the story continues to focus on Myra and her life, but it becomes more obvious that the real story is about the relationship between Myra and Helen. It is especially about what type of friend Helen proves to be.

The start of their friendship begins with Helen's description of Myra and how she is different. The first thing the reader is told about Myra is how she is laughed at for having a little brother who wets his pants. "And there was a muted giggling which alerted the rest of the class" (Munro, 162). Myra is also shown to take care of her brother and to stand with him and not get to play at recess with the rest of her class. "So Myra and Jimmy spent every recess standing in the little back porch between the two sides" (Munro, 163). So, the reader can see that Myra is nice, but she is also different from the rest of her class. Also because Helen notices all this about Myra, the reader can see that she is actually interested in her.

The moment when Helen must choose to walk beside Myra is the real place when the reader sees the conflict. Helen must choose whether to catch up to Myra and walk with her, which will look to the other kids as if they are friends. Since Myra is different and the other kids make fun of her then they might also make fun of Helen. Helen is also thinking that if she is friendly to Myra then Myra will look up to her and think she is a nice person. "I could not afford to be seen walking with her, and I did not even want to—but, on the other hand, the flattery of those humble, hopeful turnings was not lost on me" (Munro, 166). Helen does walk beside Myra, and the gift of the blue butterfly is made. This token is very important to Myra because she thinks that it means Helen is really her friend. Helen doesn't value the butterfly from the box of Cracker Jack, and she doesn't see it as very important. Helen is more interested in impressing Myra rather than in Myra's feelings. But "I realized the pledge as our fingers touched" (Munro 168). When Helen touches Myra's fingers she feels obligated to meet her early at school and talk to her at recess but then she comes to a disturbing monologue, "Why not? Why not?" (Munro, 168). Which startles a person because this girl who seems very cheerful and nice expresses prejudiced feelings.

Helen is basically a nice person, and this shows by the fact that she feels guilt or compassion for Myra. Yet, Helen never really overcomes her worry about the other kids will say if she is openly friends with Myra. This problem is removed from Helen when Myra stops coming to school. She doesn't have to decide to speak to Myra or stay with her at recess because Myra isn't there. This changes when Helen finds out that the reason Myra is not at school is because she is very sick and in the hospital. Helen has no problem in volunteering to visit her in the hospital because the idea is popular with the whole class. When the teacher asks, "So who wants to go and who wants to stay here and do supplementary reading?" (Munro, 170). "We all put up our hands" (Munro, 170). Once again Helen dodges choosing whether to be a real friend to Myra or to just follow the lead of the other kids.

There is one part of the story when Helen seems to decide. Their teacher tells about the birthday party, and Helen argues with her that Myra's real birthday is in July. Myra told her this when they talked about the butterfly pin and about birthstones. Helen was afraid of anyone learning about the butterfly pin, but now by saying this Helen is really telling the whole class that she had that conversation with Myra. A person might think Helen is standing up for Myra now, but I think she is partly just arguing with the teacher. All through the story Miss Darling is very fake, always trying to make the girls act nicely but not understanding how to do it effectively. The girls are always ignoring her or even mocking her by the way they treat Myra. So talking back to Miss Darling makes Helen just like the others.

When the chosen classmates visit Myra in the hospital they don't talk about how sick Myra really is. They act just like they are at a real birthday party, urging Myra to open presents and eat cake. When it was time for the visitors to leave, Myra called Helen back to stay for a minute. She wanted to give Helen one of her presents. "Myra said, 'I got too many things. You take something' " (Munro, 172). Helen is reluctant to take one of the gifts. Myra wants Helen to come to her house and play once she is better, but Helen can hear some kids playing outside the hospital window and only half-heartedly agrees.

Helen seems to realize that Myra's wanting her to have a gift is an act of true friendship, but the gift of the butterfly was only Helen showing off to seem like a generous person. She thinks, "I didn't want to take the case now but I couldn't think how to get out of it, what lie to tell" (Munro, 173). Helen knows that by taking the gift offered in true friendship she is saying that she is Myra's true friend. Again, Helen is relieved of having to say whether she is Myra's true friend or not. The nurse comes in and tells Helen she must leave because visiting hours are over. "So I was released, set free by the barriers which now closed about Myra . . . and by the treachery of my own heart" (Munro, 173).

Helen had only taken pity on Myra and had wanted to impress her a little, but instead she got in way over her head. Now Myra is about to die, and Helen doesn't know what to do. She never sees Myra again, but she will always remember her as the girl who just wanted a friend but couldn't have one because something held

Helen back, and Helen couldn't seem to decide what was really important. She wanted to impress the class with how like them she was, and she wanted to impress Myra with the gift of the butterfly. It is too late for Helen to change the way she acted toward Myra, but she seems to regret it very much and that is the point of this story.

GRADE

CONTENT—4

This paper gives the reader an interesting way of understanding the whole story. All of the ideas are supported with evidence from the text. The alternative idea that Helen really did become Myra's friend and stand up for her to the class is explained well.

Sometimes the writer seems to forget the question of whether Helen wants to be Myra's friend; most of the essay really explores a more interesting question, something like, "Why does Helen give Myra the butterfly pin, if she doesn't want to be her friend?" Strengthening the question at the beginning would have made for a strong paper, since the writer could have considered why Helen doesn't want to be Myra's friend, and then gone on to consider why she sometimes acts as if she did, and so gets in "over her head."

ORGANIZATION—3

Most paragraphs have clear thesis statements, although a few seem to be retelling the story. A stronger question at the beginning might have helped the writer to avoid this. The conclusion seems to be especially strong.

VOICE—4

The opening and closing paragraphs especially ring with confidence.

QUESTIONS TO REVISE STUDENT WRITING

Why does Myra interest Helen?

Why does Helen feel that there is a "pledge" between her and Myra? What do you think the pledge is? What does this pledge require of Helen?

What are Helen's prejudices against Myra?

Sample 5

In the story, "The Day of the Butterfly" by Alice Munro, Helen, a girl who is trying to be popular, can't decide whether to be friends with Myra Sayla, a girl who is very unpopular. When Helen sees that Myra is waiting for her on the road, Helen is flattered. She walks to school with Myra, shares her Cracker Jack and gives her the butterfly pin that is the prize. Helen and Myra do not become friends though because Myra becomes sick and probably dies. At the end of the story it says that Myra will become a legend. That made me wonder why such an unpopular girl would become a legend. I think it is because the reasons for her unpopularity really don't have anything to do with the real Myra.

There are a lot of reasons why Myra is unpopular. First of all, her little brother Jimmy wets his pants at school. Because he comes to her for help, everyone knows that she is related. She is the one who has to ask the teacher, "'Please may I take my brother home, he has wet himself?'" Everyone thinks that this is "shame" for Jimmy. The class giggles meanly, and the other boys in his class pick on him when he is on the playground. No one thinks that maybe Jimmy has a medical or a mental condition. Instead they just look down on him, and also on Myra. She has to spend her recess with him alone on the school porch to protect him. Because she cannot play with the other girls at recess she probably does not get to know them as well.

Also, Myra's family is poor and very sloppy. They keep a fruit store that smells like rotten fruit. Her father sits there with his shirt open, and her mother is probably cheating the customers because they have to ask the price and if they don't challenge the price she looks at them "with open mockery in her eyes." It does not sound like the store is very successful. Myra wears old women's clothes to school. She also thinks that the butterfly pin from the Cracker Jacks that Helen shares with her is very pretty and special. That shows she is from a much lower class than Gladys Healey whose father has a successful store and who wears stylish clothes.

In a way the teacher, Miss Darling, makes it worse. When Myra asks if she can take Jimmy home, the teacher makes her ask all over again, saying "accident" instead of "wet himself." Maybe Miss Darling does this because she hears the class giggle and she wants to help Myra ask in a way that won't attract attention. It is not a great idea because everyone can see what has happened. By trying to hide, it makes it seem more like it is something to be ashamed of. Myra says it "uncertainly," so probably she was embarrassed to have to ask again.

Miss Darling also makes it worse when she tells the girls to play with Myra. When she asks them why Myra does not play with them, she makes it seem like it is their fault. They think her question is "unreal" because they know a simple answer to it: "Myra has to look after her little brother." It is not a "real" question because Miss Darling is not really asking; she already thinks that the girls are being mean to Myra. Naturally the girls don't like to be blamed for Myra being on the porch. They take it out on Myra by starting the game of "Let's be nice to Myra!"

All these reasons for unpopularity don't come from Myra herself. She is very quiet and no one even notices her until her brother starts school. When she and her brother stand on the porch during recess, "Perhaps they watched the baseball games . . . perhaps they did not watch at all." They seem to be in their own little world, not worried about joining the others. The most important thing is that their faces are "uncommunicative," so the other children can't tell what they are thinking. Not caring about the others and not letting on how she feels makes Myra very different from the other girls, especially Helen, who is worried about being popular.

Helen gets a chance to meet the real Myra one day, walking to school. She catches up to Myra because Helen herself has been an unpopular girl and knows how bad it feels and it is "flattery" to see that Myra wants Helen to be with her. Also, she feels a "rush of self-conscious benevolence," she wants to show how nice she is, the way Miss Darling said. Myra is very shy; she keeps looking away from Helen and licking her lips from nervousness. But Helen does get to know her a little bit. When Myra talks about the cartoons Helen for the first time thinks about Myra doing something else than just being an outcast at school. When they find the Cracker Jack prize they have a normal conversation about colors and birthstones they like. I think Helen gives Myra the butterfly pin just because for the first time she thinks of her as a regular girl who could be a friend. Helen remembers this conversation very well because later she reminds Miss Darling that Myra's birthday is in July. Then she stands up for the real Myra when Miss Darling is just trying to be nice to the Myra no one knows.

At first the girls had a game of "being nice" to Myra. Then they have the birthday party, which is also a way of showing off how important they are and how unimportant Myra is. Myra is like "something we owned," they don't know what kind of person she really is.

Myra's legend could just be the result of the birthday party. All the girls get to feel that Myra is their "cause," and that they are being very grown up and charitable in giving her presents and treating her like a friend. They know they have been unkind to her and their presents are "guilt-tinged offerings." Her dying will make the legend even stronger, because they will never get to know her for herself. They could remember her the way she was on the school porch, apart from everyone like a statue "for worship or magic." But if Munro wanted us to think that, she would not have written the last part of the story where we see what Myra really is like.

At the birthday party Myra has a chance of showing her true self and she turns out to be the kind of person who could be popular. I expected that she would be embarrassed and would not know how to get along with the girls. But when she sees the presents, that tells her that the girls are serious in a way. She thinks they all like her, so now she can talk to them "calmly" instead of being shy. She opened the presents "with an air that not even Gladys could have bettered," and she "presided" over the whole party. She did all the birthday things just like a popular girl would. Probably all the girls will remember Myra and the way she acted like an important person. It was like magic, and that will be part of the legend for them.

At the end of the birthday party Helen sees the true difference between Myra and the other girls. Myra does not let the group dictate to her who to like. She calls Helen back to her and offers her one of her gifts, a gift that she noticed Helen admired. She insists that Helen take it, just the way Helen insisted that she take the butterfly. Also, she invites Helen over to her house to play, in a confident way. She uses her popularity to thank Helen and to try to be true friends with her. This is very different from the way Helen was, worried about what the others would think if she was friends with Myra. So Myra's legend to Helen will be an example of a true friend.

In making Myra a legend, I think Munro is trying to tell us that people are very different than they seem in the popularity race. A person like Myra can be unpopular for things that have nothing to do with them, or can suddenly get to be popular because of things that are actually bad for them, like having leukemia. Like everyone, Myra seems very different when the girls get to know her than when she was rejected as unpopular. But most people get spoiled by being popular. Myra keeps her values and still feels grateful to Helen for being friendly before. That makes her an important legend to all of us.

GRADING

CONTENT—5

This has an interesting question and explores it thoroughly. The idea that Myra's unpopularity is not caused by Myra herself is well supported; then it is superseded by the idea that Myra's own character contributes strongly to the legend. This is okay since the two ideas do not contradict each other, and they were supported by so many parts of the story, including Myra's parents and Miss Darling. Paragraph 9 gives another explanation of the legend and works it into the main idea. Finally, the paper broadens into a conclusion about popularity that is not trite.

ORGANIZATION—5

Each paragraph has a clear thesis and good support. Only paragraph 8 seems skimpy and unclear.

VOICE—4

The voice seems thoughtful and unselfconscious, although it does not especially invite the reader to join in the discussion.

QUESTIONS TO REVISE STUDENT WRITING

You point out that Miss Darling inadvertently made Myra more unpopular. Did Miss Darling also do anything to make Myra more popular through the birthday party?

Do you think that Myra's face is "uncommunicative" because she is not thinking of the others at all or because she is afraid of showing her feelings to people who tease her?

Do you think that Helen considers Myra a true friend during the story or only later when she remembers her? Why does Helen try to refuse Myra's gift?

For the Teacher

How to Use This Book

The goal of *The Reader Writes* is to teach students a process of writing powered by interpretive questioning and shared inquiry discussion. It gives students specific strategies to use at each step of the writing process, especially in the early stages of generating and thinking through ideas. Too often, inexperienced writers hurry through these stages. Later they find themselves struggling to fill paragraphs, unsure whether they have anything unique and substantial to say. *The Reader Writes* gives them concrete help.

ABOUT THE WRITER'S ROAD MAP

The Writer's Road Map (pp. 2–3) is a model of the intellectual work that goes into writing about literature. The Road Map is divided into three stages—QUESTIONS, ISSUES, and POSITIONS—each broken down into two or three steps. For each of these steps, *The Reader Writes* introduces several strategies.

As your class moves through the Writer's Road Map, they will read about and practice strategies for one stage at a time. Introducing one or two for a story is about right, if you want students to really experiment with this new way of doing things. Then, as they have incorporated those strategies into their reading and writing, they can move on to learn the strategies for the next stage.

On paper, the Road Map looks like a list to which you add strategies as you progress. As you work with them, however, you will notice that strategies from different stages are related or even overlap. After all, thinking is not like building with bricks, adding chunk to chunk to make a whole. It is much more like modeling with clay, shaping and reshaping to gradually refine a finished piece.

You can see this shaping and refining process very clearly if you compare the essay assignments for each stage. An Open Question, Exploring an Issue, and Arguing for a Position are all full essays. As your students go through the stages, they do not add parts to their previous essays; instead they develop and refine each part. They move from a broad topic question to a definite thesis. They shape rough answers to that question into supported answers and then into a thesis that is explored with interrelated, well-developed ideas.

So encourage your students to follow the Road Map as a way to learn and remember strategies that can help them to shape their thoughts, and look forward to the time when they move readily from stage to stage, dipping back or reaching forward as their thinking requires.

GETTING STARTED

The easiest way to start is to choose a story, then work on the strategies connected with that story. For instance, if you pick "Harrison Bergeron" you will use Hurry Up/Slow Down as your Reading to Question strategy. Next explore A Question Chart as your Sharing Questions strategy. Finally, have a shared inquiry discussion and assign Writing: An Open Question, the essay assignment for QUESTIONS.

Your next story might be "At Her Father's and Her Mother's Place," for which you will introduce the Patterns and Interpretive Questions strategies. Again, your essay assignment will be An Open Question, since you are still in the QUESTIONS stage.

For ISSUES, choose stories connected with the ISSUES strategies. First lead students through QUESTIONS, applying the previously explored strategies to the new story. Then start on the new strategies connected with the story you've selected. Finally, in POSITIONS, start again with QUESTIONS strategies, followed by ISSUES strategies, and then introduce the POSITIONS strategies connected with your new story.

PLANNING CLASS TIME FOR WORK ON EACH STORY

For each story and essay, plan to spend a week to a week and a half. Teaching each strategy in the Writer's Action Plan will take one or two class periods, or a class period and a homework assignment. You'll need time for students to read about the strategy and review the demo, and then practice the new strategy themselves. You will want to give your students time to employ the strategies fully, yet keep the pace from dragging.

QUESTIONS
A PLAN FOR EACH STORY AND ESSAY

Reading for Questions

Introduce and practice the strategy	one class period
Complete reading and notes	one class period or homework

Sharing Questions

Introduce and practice the strategy	one class period

Shared Inquiry Discussion

one class period for each group (preferably, discussion groups are 10–15 students)

Prepare to write

one class period

Draft the essay

one or two class periods or homework

ISSUES
A PLAN FOR EACH STORY AND ESSAY

Reading to Question

Apply the strategies independently — one class period or homework

Sharing Questions

Apply the strategies in collaboration — one class period

Searching for Evidence

Introduce and practice the strategy — one class period

Complete note taking — one class period or homework

Shared Inquiry Discussion

Introduce and practice the strategy — one class period for each group

Plan the essay, introduce and practice the strategy — one class period

Draft the essay — one or two class periods or homework

POSITIONS
A PLAN FOR EACH STORY AND ESSAY

Reading to Question

Apply the strategies independently — one class period or homework

Sharing Questions

Apply the strategies in collaboration — one class period

Searching for Evidence

Apply the strategies independently — one or two class periods or homework

Shared Inquiry Discussion

Apply the strategies in collaboration — one class period for each group

Crafting a Position

Introduce and practice the strategy — one or two class periods or homework

Nailing it Down

Introduce and practice the strategy — one or two class periods or homework

Draft the essay — one or two class periods or homework

Testing It

Introduce and practice the strategy — one class period

Rewrite — one or two class periods or homework

Students often want to move more quickly through the writing process, and as they learn the strategies, they can do so. But students commonly spend too little time rather than too much time working through their ideas before writing. Help them see the value of serious preparation for writing.

TEACHING A STRATEGY

The strategies are the heart of *The Reader Writes*. To teach them effectively

* Read or review the introduction to the numbered step.

* Read the strategy description and the demo with your students.

* Talk through how you would use the strategy, with examples. Have students talk through how they would complete the demo.

* Lead students in a brief practice session of the strategy, each thinking out loud about how he or she would apply it.

* Ask students to try out the strategy. For group activities like discussion, model the strategy yourself as you lead the class.

Let students know you are standing by for individual coaching.

DISCUSSION AND QUESTIONING ACTIVITIES

Expert writers seldom work alone. They have colleagues, editors, and others with whom to talk over their ideas. Your students should, too.

In Sharing Questions, the whole class is a sounding board for finding questions about a story. In Shared Inquiry Discussion, everyone's ideas are clarified and supported. Later, when students have captured ideas in written notes, outlines, or drafts, a partner or two can be the best help for thinking through their work.

Questioning is the key to each of these activities. Questions show a writer where you don't understand his or her thinking, without critiquing his or her ideas or substituting your own. Questioning can give your students concrete examples of the kind of thinking you want them to do. So give the questioning strategies included in *The Reader Writes* as much attention as the paper and pencil strategies. Model them yourself in large- and small-group activities and encourage your students to use them in discussions and when they coach each other.

ASSIGNING WRITING TOPICS

The Reader Writes teaches students how to generate questions that become their own essay topics. This is a challenging process. If you give an assignment based on your own interpretive question or other prompt, your students probably will produce an essay more quickly. But will they learn more quickly how to write?

To develop interesting, well-supported ideas, students need an active, probing curiosity. They have to know how to explore a reading thoroughly to find the issues in it. Answering an assigned topic or question *tests* these skills, but does not necessarily *develop* them.

When students must find their own topics, they learn to probe for issues—to be deliberately curious. It will take time, but with practice your students will gain a stronger sense of themselves as readers and writers, as well as the skills to meet any literacy task with confident engagement.

USING JOURNALS

Journals can structure the habit of writing in stages. Have your students keep a writer's journal for all their work for *The Reader Writes*—first notes about the story, early drafts of questions, class notes from Sharing Questions. Self-stick notes and notecards can be stapled to pages or collected in a pocket.

Ask them to show their work when they turn in their essay drafts. Look over their journals and coach them on including all steps and keeping their notes in order. Point out the growth of thought you see in a well-kept journal.

ASSESSING STUDENTS' WRITING

The grading rubrics for *The Reader Writes* are based on the Six Traits, with a special focus on content, organization, and voice. At each stage, a rubric spells out achievement levels based on the strategies you've taught. You can use them to grade rigorously and also to judge whether students are ready to move on to the next stage. Emphasizing content, organization, and voice as you grade will show your students a clear match between their paper grades and their classwork.

If you already use a different rubric or checklist for expository or persuasive writing, you can combine it with the *The Reader Writes* rubrics by treating the descriptions of content and organization as a more detailed description of content, thesis, and support. Again, give these objectives extra weight in calculating a grade.

The Reader Writes grading rubrics include a seventh trait, Process for Thinking and Writing. Since *The Reader Writes* is organized around a writing process, it makes sense to review students' journals and drafts to assess how well that process is working for them. You might comment on journals informally while you coach students at work writing their drafts, you might collect and read journals at set times, or you might ask that journals be available in portfolios. It's less important to give a grade than to show students how much good notes and reflections can contribute to essays that truly reflect their thinking.

TEACHING SENTENCE STRUCTURE, GRAMMAR, STYLE, AND MECHANICS

The writing assignments include Conventions to Master that will make it easier for your students to express their ideas accurately in writing. You can handle these separately, in units between stories or between stages, or you can integrate them as mini-lessons during class periods while students are taking notes or drafting their homework. As you teach conventions, add them to your grading rubrics.

ADAPTING TO STUDENTS' ABILITIES

The Writer's Road Map gives you and your students a picture of the whole writing process, with starting points and goals showing where your students should be when they start a strategy and where they should end up.

For instance, students beginning Searching for Evidence must have interpretive questions, developed during QUESTIONS. Without the interpretive questions that form their topics, they can't find evidence for possible answers.

As your students work on a story unit, assess which goals are harder for them and plan to give them more time to practice the appropriate strategies. If they struggle to develop good questions, continue to work at the QUESTIONS stage using later stories. On the other hand, if your group finds writing questions a snap, move on to ISSUES. Assign the stories used for demos in the ISSUES stage or adapt ISSUES strategies to earlier stories.

Because *The Reader Writes* is arranged by strategies rather than by stories, you can easily select strategies according to your students' needs. If a strategy is not demonstrated with a story you want to use, skip the written demo and demonstrate the strategy using the story you've selected. Ways to demo include

* Talking through how you would use the strategy

* Thinking out loud as you use the strategy on passages from your story

* Writing up examples so students see the steps of the process and the results

* Leading your students in using the strategy as a group, then posting their work

Novice writers will master the process best if they deliberately practice strategies. Structure class time to encourage them to practice strategies from early stages. At first this will seem artificial. Gradually, they will use more and more strategies on their own. Eventually they will learn to move through the stages without interrupting the flow, as skilled writers do.

APPLYING STRATEGIES TO OTHER READING SELECTIONS

The Writer's Road Map fits all challenging, interesting literature. Your students should transfer these strategies to other stories, as well as novels and plays.

The Junior Great Books stories are rich in meaning, chosen for depth and multidimensionality. Such literature makes it easier for readers to ask many questions that go somewhere and to find many interesting answers to their questions. Beginning writers especially need the support this depth gives them. Also, because Series 7 opens with shorter stories and builds to "Diary of a Young Girl" and *A Christmas Carol,* your students will move naturally into working with longer texts.

But strategy learning is all about transference, using strategies in situations different from those in which you learned them. So you can extend each stage with work on a novel, play, longer poem, or memoir. Or, use *The Reader Writes* for your short-story unit and then apply the strategies to novels or plays later in the school year.

READING AND DISCUSSING STORIES WITHOUT ASSIGNING WRITING

Of course you can read and discuss some stories without a paper assignment. Your students will appreciate the variety! You can treat the steps in QUESTIONS and ISSUES as reading activities, then hold a shared inquiry discussion as the culminating activity. Or, use activities from the Series 7 Leader's Guide.

If you have questions or comments about *The Reader Writes,* please contact the Great Books Foundation at 1-800-222-5870. We value your feedback.

The Reader Writes addresses many of the standards most frequently required of language arts programs. The chart below shows alignment with the Mid-Continent Regional Education Laboratory (MCREL) Language Arts Standards. The MCREL standards have been compiled from state standards, so you will be able to identify your own state standards in the list.

THE WRITER'S ROAD MAP		MCREL STANDARDS: LANGUAGE ARTS	
STAGES	**STRATEGIES**		
Questions	Reading for Questions	5:1	Establishes and adjusts purposes for reading
		5:4	Uses specific strategies to clear up confusing parts of a text
	Sharing Questions	5:6	Reflects on what has been learned after reading and formulates ideas, opinions, and personal responses to texts
		8:1	Plays a variety of roles in group discussions
		8:2	Asks questions to seek elaboration and clarification of ideas
	Writing: An Open Question	1:1	Prewriting: Uses a variety of prewriting strategies
		1:2	Drafting and Revising: Uses a variety of strategies to draft and revise written work
		1:12	Writes in response to literature
		2:2	Uses paragraph form in writing
Issues	Searching for Evidence	1:1	Prewriting: Uses a variety of prewriting strategies
		5:1	Establishes and adjusts purposes for reading
		5:4	Uses specific strategies to clear up confusing parts of a text
	Shared Inquiry Discussion	5:6	Reflects on what has been learned after reading and formulates ideas, opinions, and personal responses to texts
		8:1	Plays a variety of roles in group discussions
		8:2	Asks questions to seek elaboration and clarification of ideas
		8:3	Uses strategies to enhance listening comprehension
		8:5	Conveys a clear main point when speaking to others and stays on the topic being discussed
	Writing: Exploring an Issue	1:2	Drafting and Revising: Uses a variety of strategies to draft and revise written work
		1:12	Writes in response to literature
		2:2	Uses paragraph form in writing
Positions	Crafting a Position	1:1	Prewriting: Uses a variety of prewriting strategies
	Nailing It Down	1:2	Drafting and Revising: Uses a variety of strategies to draft and revise written work

	Writing: Arguing for a Position	1:6	Writes expository compositions
		1:12	Writes in response to literature
		2:2	Uses paragraph form in writing
		2:4	Uses explicit transitional devices
	Testing It	1:2	Drafting and Revising: Uses a variety of strategies to draft and revise written work
		1:4	Evaluates own and others' writing
		8:2	Asks questions to seek elaboration and clarification of ideas
All stages	All strategies	6:1–12	Uses reading skills and strategies to understand and interpret a variety of literary texts

Questions

Teacher's Plan

Photocopy this form and use it to plan your class's work on each story.

❏ Harrison Bergeron

❏ I Just Kept On Smiling

❏ At Her Father's and Her Mother's Place

1. READING FOR QUESTIONS

Strategy: _____   Day/period: _____

2. SHARING QUESTIONS

Strategy: _____   Day/period: _____

SHARED INQUIRY DISCUSSION (p. 22)   Day/period: _____

WRITING: AN OPEN QUESTION (p. 24)   Day/period: _____

NOTES ON STUDENTS' PROGRESS:

_____

_____

_____

_____

Issues

Teacher's Plan

Photocopy this form and use it to plan your class's work on each story.

- ❑ The White Circle
- ❑ End of the Game
- ❑ The Zodiacs
- ❑ The Cat and the Coffee Drinkers

1. READING FOR QUESTIONS

Strategy: _____   Day/period: _____

2. SHARING QUESTIONS

Strategy: _____   Day/period: _____

3. SEARCHING FOR EVIDENCE

Strategy: _____   Day/period: _____

4. SHARED INQUIRY DISCUSSION

Strategy: _____   Day/period: _____

WRITING: EXPLORING AN ISSUE (p. 54)   Day/period: _____

NOTES ON STUDENTS' PROGRESS:

_____

_____

_____

_____

Positions

Teacher's Plan

Photocopy this form and use it to plan your class's work on each story.

❑ The Diary of a Young Girl   ❑ The Secret Lion

❑ Day of the Butterfly   ❑ A Christmas Carol

1. READING FOR QUESTIONS

    Strategy: _____   Day/period: _____

2. SHARING QUESTIONS

    Strategy: _____   Day/period: _____

3. SEARCHING FOR EVIDENCE

    Strategy: _____   Day/period: _____

4. SHARED INQUIRY DISCUSSION

    Strategy: _____   Day/period: _____

5. CRAFTING A POSITION

    Strategy: _____   Day/period: _____

6. NAILING IT DOWN

    Strategy: _____   Day/period: _____

WRITING: A POSITION ESSAY (p. 85)   Day/period: _____

7. TESTING IT

    Strategy: _____   Day/period: _____